Victoria Crosses of the Zulu and Boer Wars

Victoria Crosses of the Zulu and Boer Wars

Kevin Brazier

Pen & Sword
MILITARY

First published in Great Britain in 2021 by
Pen & Sword Military
An imprint of
Pen & Sword Books Ltd
Yorkshire – Philadelphia

Copyright © Kevin Brazier 2021

ISBN 978 1 39909 913 4

The right of Kevin Brazier to be identified as Author of this work has been asserted by him in accordance with the Copyright, Designs and Patents Act 1988.

A CIP catalogue record for this book is
available from the British Library.

All rights reserved. No part of this book may be reproduced or transmitted in any form or by any means, electronic or mechanical including photocopying, recording or by any information storage and retrieval system, without permission from the Publisher in writing.

Typeset by Mac Style
Printed and bound by CPI Group (UK) Ltd, Croydon, CR0 4YY

Pen & Sword Books Limited incorporates the imprints of Atlas, Archaeology, Aviation, Discovery, Family History, Fiction, History, Maritime, Military, Military Classics, Politics, Select, Transport, True Crime, Air World, Frontline Publishing, Leo Cooper, Remember When, Seaforth Publishing, The Praetorian Press, Wharncliffe Local History, Wharncliffe Transport, Wharncliffe True Crime and White Owl.

For a complete list of Pen & Sword titles please contact

PEN & SWORD BOOKS LIMITED
47 Church Street, Barnsley, South Yorkshire, S70 2AS, England
E-mail: enquiries@pen-and-sword.co.uk
Website: www.pen-and-sword.co.uk

Or

PEN AND SWORD BOOKS
1950 Lawrence Rd, Havertown, PA 19083, USA
E-mail: Uspen-and-sword@casematepublishers.com
Website: www.penandswordbooks.com

For Andrew, a good friend whom I will miss.

Contents

Acknowledgements ix
Author's Note x

Part 1: The Zulu War 1

Chapter 1	iSandlwana	3
Chapter 2	Rorke's Drift	9
Chapter 3	Intombe River	39
Chapter 4	Hlobane Mountain and Khambula	41
Chapter 5	Ulundi	54

Part 2: The First Boer War 59

| Chapter 6 | Elandsfontein, Laing's Nek, Wasselstroom and Mujaba Mountain | 61 |

Part 3: The Second Boer War 69

Chapter 7	Siege of Mafeking and Ladysmith	71
Chapter 8	Magersfontein and Colenso	83
Chapter 9	Colesberg and Relief of Ladysmith	98
Chapter 10	Paardeberg	105
Chapter 11	Onderbank Spruit, Plewman's Farm, Hart's Hill and the Tugela Heights	107
Chapter 12	Bloemfontein and Korn Spruit	112
Chapter 13	Wakkerstroom, Crow's Nest Hill, Delagoa Bay Railway, Lindley, Wolve Spruit and Krugersdorp	120
Chapter 14	Vredefort, Mosilikatse Nek, Essenbosch Farm, Van Wyk's Vlei, Geluk and Bergendal	131

Chapter 15	Warm Baths, Geluk, Zeerust, Komati River, Dewetsdorp and Nooitgedacht Hill	138
Chapter 16	Monument Hill, Naauwpoort, Bothwell Camp, Strijdenburg and Derby	149
Chapter 17	Brakpan, Lambrechtfontein, Thaba 'Nchu, Vlakfontein, Springbok Laagte, Ruiter's Kraal, Blood River, Itala, Moedwil, Geelhoutboom, Tygerkloof Spruit, Tafelkop and Vlakfontein	155

Glossary   173
Bibliography   175
Alphabetical List   176

Acknowledgements

First, I'd like to thank Rupert Harding for commissioning me to write this book, and Linne Matthews for her excellent job of checking my work. Jill Sugden, for her many hours of proofreading, Mark Green, for his continued support and research, also for access to his excellent website and photo archive, which can be found at: www.vconline.org.uk. All grave photos are from the author's collection. I must also mention the Victoria Cross Trust for their continued support; check out their website at: www.victoriacrosstrust.org. Finally, for all those who gave up their knowledge in forums and historical groups such as on Facebook, in particular Ian Knight and James Bancroft. For further updates and new projects, friend me on Facebook: search Kevin Brazier Author.

Author's Note

A number of the VCs recorded in this book were awarded to soldiers involved in the same action. In order to set each individual's VC action in context, some of the general details of the operation concerned have been repeated in several entries.

Part 1

The Zulu War

Imperial fever was growing in Britain, and in 1877, to secure the stability of lands contested by both Britain and the Boers, a high commissioner was sent to create a federal dominion of British Colonies and Boer Republics. To do this he needed to control the land bordering Natal and the Transvaal, which belonged to the Zulus. The Zulu king, Cetshwayo, refused to give up this land. Britain needed a reason to invade Zululand, so Sir Henry Bartle Frere, High Commissioner for Southern Africa (1877–80), along with Lord Chelmsford, sent an ultimatum (without the permission or knowledge of the government in England) ordering Cetshwayo to disband his army, something they knew he would not do, so when this was ignored, war was imminent. Twenty-three Victoria Crosses were awarded for this campaign.

Chapter 1

iSandlwana

Teignmouth MELVILL, iSandlwana, 22 January 1879

Teignmouth Melvill was born on 8 September 1842 in Marylebone, London, the son of Philip Melvill, Military Secretary to the East India Company. He was educated at Harrow, from 1856 to 1858, and Cambridge University, graduating with a BA in 1865. He joined the army the same year with a purchase as ensign and became lieutenant by purchase in 1868.

Teignmouth Melvill.

Melvill proceeded with his regiment to Malta and then to Gibraltar. While there, in April 1874 he joined the Lodge of Friendship. In September the same year, his colleague Nevill Coghill also joined the Friendship. Both men called off their Friendship prior to leaving the garrison. Early in 1875, Melvill's battalion was ordered to the Cape Colony, where he took part in the bush fighting at Griqualand West. In 1876 he married Sara Elizabeth, daughter of George Thomas Reed of Port Elizabeth, in the Cape, and they went on to have two children.

In 1877 there was an outbreak of unrest among the Gaika and Gcaleka tribes around the north-eastern border of the Cape Colony. The 1st Battalion was sent to deal with the inter-tribal fighting and after a series of skirmishes to flush the natives out of the bush, the Gcaleka chief, Kreli, was captured. In June 1878, Sandile, chief of the Gaikas, was killed; the rebels lost heart and the fighting ended.

Melvill passed the exam for entry into the Staff College at Camberley but obtained permission to stay as adjutant of the 1st Battalion, 24th Foot for the coming campaign against the Zulus. Attached to No. 3 Column of the 24th, he crossed the Buffalo River on 11 January 1879 and took part in the first action of the war at the stronghold of Chief Sihayo in the Batshe River Valley. Then, on 20 January, the 1st Battalion camped at the base of iSandlwana.

Early on the morning of the 22nd, Lord Chelmsford took half of the force to look for the Zulus and to locate another camp site. Left behind were six companies of the 24th, two field guns and the Natal Native Contingent (NNC), who would join Chelmsford once the new camp site was selected. Lieutenant Colonel Anthony Durnford arrived at the camp at about 10.30 am, becoming the senior officer in the camp. He was told by Lieutenant Colonel Henry Pulleine that Zulus had been seen on the iNyoni escarpment and he had the men fall in, but the warriors had now withdrawn and they were stood down. Shortly after 11.00 am, Durnford left the camp to scout for the Zulu army. Around midday, the Zulus launched their attack using the classic 'buffalo horns' formation, with which they were able to outflank the British firing line.

As the line began to collapse, Lieutenant Melvill tried to save the Queen's Regimental Colour. (It is impossible to say whether he was ordered to do so by Pulleine or did this on his own initiative, but as adjutant, the colour was his responsibility. He may have intended to use the flag as a rally point.) En route from the camp he was joined by Lieutenant Coghill and they rode together, pursued by Zulu warriors, to the swollen Buffalo River. Coghill crossed safely, but Melvill was being carried away by the torrent. As Coghill plunged back into the river to assist his comrade, his horse was shot from under him. Both men struggled to the Natal bank, where they were engulfed by Zulus. When their bodies

The grave of Teignmouth Melvill and Nevill Coghill at Fugitives' Drift.

were discovered, a ring of dead Zulus was found all around them. The colour was found ten days later downstream.

Teignmouth Melvill is buried with Nevill Coghill at Fugitives' Drift, below Itchiane Hill, in the KwaZulu-Natal province of South Africa. At the time of their deaths, the VC was not awarded posthumously (although there is nothing in the Victoria Cross Royal Warrant to this effect, it had been practice not to do so), but in 1907 a number of backdated awards were granted by King Edward VII, including Melvill's. His VC is held by the Regimental Museum of the Royal Welsh, in Brecon, Powys.

Nevill Josiah Aylmer COGHILL, iSandlwana, 22 January 1879

Nevill Coghill.

Nevill Coghill was born on 25 January 1852 in Drumcondra, County Dublin, Ireland, the eldest son of Sir John Joscelyn Coghill, 4th Baronet, JP, DL, of Drumcondra, and his wife the Hon. Katherine Francis Plunket. He was educated at Haileybury (Trevelyan, 1865–69) before joining the army as an ensign in 1873.

He was posted first to Malta and then to Gibraltar. While there, along with his colleague Teignmouth Melvill, he joined the Lodge of Friendship in September 1874, but they both called off their Friendship prior to leaving the garrison. Early in 1875, his battalion was ordered to the Cape Colony, but Coghill returned to the new depot at Brecon. In August 1875 he was commissioned a lieutenant in the 1st Battalion, 24th Regiment of Foot.

Coghill sailed to South Africa to join his battalion in January 1876, and in August was appointed ADC to General Sir Arthur Cunynghame GOC British troops in South Africa. He accompanied the general on a grand tour of inspection throughout the region. Coghill fought in a number of skirmishes during the Ninth Cape Frontier War and was mentioned in despatches in January 1878. He sailed home with General

Cunynghame when he was replaced by Lord Chelmsford in March 1878, but after some leave, Coghill returned to South Africa.

He was appointed ADC to Sir Henry Bartle Frere, Governor of the Cape, but was given permission to join his battalion for the coming war with the Zulus, joining No. 3 Column as an orderly officer to Colonel Richard Glyn. The 24th crossed the Buffalo River on 11 January 1879 and Coghill took part in the first action of the war at the stronghold of Chief Sihayo in the Batshe River Valley. Then, on 20 January, the 1st Battalion camped at the base of iSandlwana. Coghill accompanied Chelmsford on a reconnaissance, during which he twisted his knee and spent the following day laid up. Early on the morning of the 22nd, Lord Chelmsford took half of the force to look for the Zulus and to locate another camp site. Left behind were six companies of the 24th, two field guns and the NNC, who would join him once the new camp site was selected. Lieutenant Colonel Durnford arrived at the camp at about 10.30 am, becoming the senior officer in the camp. He was told by Lieutenant Colonel Pulleine that Zulus had been seen on the iNyoni escarpment and he had the men fall in, but the warriors had now withdrawn and they were stood down. Shortly after 11.00 am Durnford left the camp to scout for the Zulu army. Around midday, the Zulus launched their attack using the classic buffalo horns formation, with which they were able to outflank the British firing line. As the line was falling back, Coghill rode into camp and told Colonel Glyn's groom to strike the tents and take the colonel's horse to the rear.

During the rout Coghill joined Lieutenant Melvill, who was carrying the Queen's Colour of their regiment to safety. Together they rode, pursued by Zulu warriors, to the swollen Buffalo River. Coghill crossed safely, but Melvill was being carried away by the torrent. As Coghill plunged back into the river to assist his comrade, his horse was shot from under him. Both men struggled to the Natal bank, where they were engulfed by Zulus. When their bodies were discovered, a ring of dead Zulus was found all around them. The colour was found ten days later downstream.

Nevill Coghill is buried with Teignmouth Melvill at Fugitives' Drift, below Itchiane Hill, South Africa. At the time of their deaths, the VC was not awarded posthumously (although there is nothing in the Victoria Cross Warrant to this effect, it had been practice not to do so) but in 1907 a number of backdated awards were granted by King Edward VII, including Coghill's. His VC is held by the Regimental Museum of the Royal Welsh, Brecon, Powys.

Samuel WASSALL, iSandlwana, 22 January 1879

Samuel Wassall was born on 28 July 1856 in Aston, Birmingham, the son of Thomas Wassall, a wire worker, and Elizabeth (née Silk). In November 1874 he enlisted into the 80th Regiment of Foot (later the South Staffordshire Regiment), giving his job as a silk dyer.

In 1874, three companies of his regiment were sent to Singapore as reinforcements to deal with the murderers of the Governor of the Perak Province. The fighting did not last long and his unit returned to Hong Kong. From there he sailed to Mauritius in the Indian Ocean, but en route measles broke out among the children and the ship was diverted to the Cape Colony. Due to the sickness they were refused permission to land until 6 March 1876. Wassall's company was sent to join Colonel Hugh Rowlands VC for an expedition against Chief Sekhukhune and the Pedi tribe. However, due to a serious drought, the expedition was called off.

Samuel Wassall.

Wassall's company (now acting as mounted infantry) was sent to Rorke's Drift to join No. 3 Column. He took part in the attack on the stronghold of Chief Sihayo in the Batshe River Valley. Then, on 20 January, they encamped at the base of iSandlwana.

Around midday on the 22nd, the Zulus launched their attack using the classic buffalo horns formation, with which they were able to outflank the British firing line. As the line began to collapse it became every man for himself and Wassall was being pursued towards the swollen Buffalo River. He spurred his horse into the river and was making his way across when he saw Private Thomas Westwood (of the 80th Regiment) being swept away by the water. Wassall returned to the Zulu side, dismounted, leaving his horse, and helped Westwood by dragging him out of the river. He remounted his horse, and with Westwood riding behind him crossed to the Natal side under a heavy shower of bullets and spears.

After visiting Rorke's Drift and meeting Lord Chelmsford, who told him 'You are a lucky man to have got away', Wassall moved to Khambula with the mounted infantry and, after the Battle of Hlobane, took part in operations with Colonel Evelyn Wood's Flying Column and was present at the Battle of Ulundi. He returned to iSandlwana in May and was asked to recount his experience there. His VC, gazetted on 17 June 1879, was presented to him by Lord Wolseley at Utrecht on 11 September 1879.

Wassall left the army in 1880 and settled in Barrow-in-Furness in Cumbria, where he married Rebecca Round, and they went on to have four sons and three daughters. He met George V and Queen Mary in May 1917. He was invited to attend a garden party with 300 other VC recipients on 26 June 1920 at Buckingham Palace and Rebecca said it was one of the greatest experiences of her life.

Samuel Wassall died on 31 January 1927 and is buried in Barrow-in-Furness Cemetery, Section 3.B, Plot 1952. His VC is held by the Staffordshire Regiment Museum, Lichfield. His descendant, Genial Wassall, is a veteran of the Falklands War and the first Gulf War in Iraq, where he was commended for his bravery by General Norman Schwarzkopf.

Chapter 2

Rorke's Drift

John Rouse Merriott CHARD, Rorke's Drift, 22/23 January 1879

John Chard.

John Chard was born on 21 December 1847 in Boxhill, near Plymouth, one of three sons and four daughters of William Wheaton Chard and his wife Jane (née Brimacombe). His older brother William Wheaton Chard served with the Royal Fusiliers, rising to the rank of colonel, while his younger brother Charles Edward Chard became rector of the parish church in Hatch Beauchamp, Somerset. John Chard was educated at Plymouth New Grammar School, and had private tutorship before entering the Royal Military Academy at Woolwich, where he was remembered for always being late for breakfast.

Chard was commissioned lieutenant in the Royal Engineers on 15 July 1868, and after two years of instruction he sailed to Bermuda in 1870, being employed in the building of fortifications at Hamilton Dockyard. He returned to England for his father's funeral in January 1874, and was posted to Malta the following month, where he was engaged in building defences. Chard returned to England in April 1876, where, after a short stay at Chatham, he was posted to the 5th Company, Royal Engineers.

He set sail for South Africa on 2 December 1879, arriving at Durban on 5 January, where he received orders to join No. 3 Column with a small party of engineers. The roads were very poor and they did not get to Rorke's Drift until 19 January. Almost at once he set to work improving the ponts across the river.

On the morning of 22 January 1879, Chard received orders to take a party of engineers to iSandlwana. However, on his arrival he was informed that only his men were required and that he should return to Rorke's Drift. While at iSandlwana Chard saw the Zulu army approaching and on his return reported this to Major Henry Spalding, the garrison commander at Rorke's Drift, at about 1.00 pm. Spalding decided to go to Helpmekaar to hurry up a company that was meant to be taking over from B Company to garrison the station but were overdue. He checked the Army List, which confirmed that Chard was senior to Gonville Bromhead, and he informed him of this, saying, 'I'll be back this afternoon, early; I don't suppose anything will happen.' Chard returned to his camp by the ponts.

Shortly after 3.00 pm, while Chard was catching up on his correspondence his attention was brought to two horsemen galloping towards him from the Zulu side of the river. One of them was Lieutenant Adendorff of the NNC, who informed him that the camp at iSandlwana had been overrun and all the men killed. Soon after, a message from Bromhead arrived asking him to return to the post immediately. On his arrival Chard found the preparations for defence were underway. Bromhead informed him that a large body of Zulus was advancing on their position and they were ordered to hold at all costs. After a brief consultation with his fellow officers Chard agreed with the arrangements, particularly with the hospital being taken into the defence perimeter. He returned to the river, where the men suggested they could moor the ponts midstream and defend them from there, but Chard ordered them to return to the mission station with him. Once back at the station Chard moved about the perimeter suggesting improvements and seeing that every man knew his place.

At about 4.20 pm, the first wave of Zulus was seen approaching the post, which sparked a mass desertion of the colonial troops, leaving a little over 150 men to man the perimeter. Chard realised that his line of defence was too long and quickly ordered a row of biscuit boxes to be placed from the corner of the storehouse to the north wall.

At 4.30 pm the Zulus came on, attacking the south barricade and hospital building. Their first rush was soon stopped, and the warriors moved to their left, around the hospital, and attacked from the north-west. After some time they gained entry and Chard ordered Bromhead to lead a counter-attack to throw them out. Six times the Zulus broke in, and six times Bromhead led a bayonet charge to restore the situation. At the same time, the Zulus were still attacking the hospital building and managed to gain entry, as well setting the thatch roof alight. Realising that the position could not be held, Chard ordered the men to fall back to the biscuit box position, leaving the hospital building under attack and surrounded. As darkness fell, the fire from the hospital roof gave the garrison enough light to see the warriors charging in, enabling them to pour a deadly fire into the masses of men.

At about 7.00 pm, Chard ordered a final redoubt to be built from two piles of mealie bags in front of the store (this work may have already been started by Assistant Commissariat Walter Dunne). He had all of the wounded and some of the men placed inside, just in time to meet the final Zulu onslaught. Attacking from the north-east, the Zulus had to charge through a rough stone cattle kraal and over a rocky ledge, and force their way into another kraal defended by the garrison, which they almost succeeded in doing, but as the night wore on the attacks became less frequent and the warriors were reduced to a desultory fire.

The garrison had to remain alert throughout the night in case of any sudden Zulu attacks, but by 4.30 am the next morning, the warriors could be seen withdrawing to the south-west. Unsure if this was a feint, Chard kept the men busy repairing the barricades. Relief came at about 7.00 am when Lord Chelmsford arrived with the remains of his column.

For his conduct during the battle Chard was mentioned in despatches and awarded the Victoria Cross, gazetted on 2 May 1879. He was promoted to captain and brevet major, backdated to 23 January 1879. It was noted in his despatches that 'he has spoken of everyone but himself'.

Chard remained at Rorke's Drift, working on building a more secure stone fort (later named Fort Bromhead) and supervising the burial of the Zulu dead, reporting the number as 351. However, conditions were poor and he fell ill with fever and in February was taken to Ladysmith for treatment. He was showing signs of improvement but suffered a relapse and in May it was falsely reported that he had died. After his recovery he was assigned to Colonel Wood's Flying Column at Khambula to improve the fortifications. He remained with Wood's column during the advance to Ulundi, following Colonel Redvers Buller's reconnaissances, and building bridges and repairing roads. Chard was present at the Battle of Ulundi, witnessing the final defeat of the Zulus. He was presented with his VC by Lord Wolseley at St Paul's Church in KwaZulu Natal, South Africa, on 16 July 1879.

Chard returned to England on board HMS *Eagle*, arriving at Spithead on 2 October 1879, where the Duke of Cambridge delivered a message from the Queen inviting him to an audience with her at Balmoral. Chard was presented with a sword of honour and a gold watch at Plymouth as 'The Hero of Rorke's Drift,' also receiving an illuminated address from the Exeter Freemasons. Many other honours were to follow; he was held in high esteem in the West Country for the remainder of his life.

Chard was invited to Balmoral again in February 1880, when he gave Queen Victoria a more detailed account of the Battle of Rorke's Drift. In December 1881 he was posted to Cyprus, where his brevet majority was substantiated in July 1886. He returned to England in March 1887 to take up a position at Fulwood Barracks, Preston, where the Reverend George Smith ('Ammunition Smith', as he became known due to his work at Rorke's Drift) was stationed.

On 14 December 1892, Chard sailed for Singapore, where he was Acting Commander Royal Engineer, being promoted to lieutenant colonel on 8 January 1893. He returned home in January 1896 and was appointed Commander Royal Engineer at Perth, Scotland. In the following May he presented Queen Victoria with Japanese mementoes he had brought back especially for her. Chard was promoted to colonel on 8 January 1897.

Chard, a long-time pipe smoker, was diagnosed with cancer of the tongue and he underwent two operations, the second to remove his tongue, although it was said he could still converse clearly. Reverend Smith visited him, and the Duke of Connaught, Lord Chelmsford and Queen Victoria all sent telegrams enquiring about his condition. Placed on the army sick list in August 1897, John Chard died on 1 November that year at Hatch Beauchamp.

Chard's grave, St John the Baptist churchyard, Hatch Beauchamp, Somerset.

John Chard was buried with full military honours at St John the Baptist churchyard, Hatch Beauchamp, Somerset. As well as wreaths from officers of the South Wales Borderers, there were tributes from Colonel Edward Browne VC and the Queen, with a note in her own hand saying: 'A mark of admiration and regard for a brave soldier from his sovereign.' Chard's VC (once owned by the actor Stanley Baker, although it was only proved to be the original after his death) is now in the Ashcroft Gallery at the Imperial War Museum, London.

Gonville 'Gunny' or 'Gonny' BROMHEAD, Rorke's Drift, 22/23 January 1879

Gonville Bromhead.

Gonville Bromhead was born on 29 August 1845 in Versailles, France, into a distinguished military family. He was the ninth of ten children born to Major Edmund de Gonville Bromhead, 3rd Baronet, and his wife Judith Christine Cahill, daughter of James Wood, of Woodville, County Sligo, Ireland. His uncle was commander of the 77th Regiment at El Bodon in 1811, leading the men in a successful assault against the French Cavalry. His father fought as a lieutenant with the 54th Regiment at Waterloo, losing an eye, and later led the 'forlorn hope' during the storming of Cambrai. His grandfather, Sir Gonville Bromhead, was a lieutenant general who distinguished himself in Burgoyne's Campaign and was captured at Saratoga in 1777, and his great-grandfather, Boardman Bromhead, served as ensign under Wolfe at Quebec in 1759. It is believed to have been he who informed the dying general that the French were retreating.

Gonville's oldest brother, Edward, fought in the Crimean War and died in Burma serving with the 76th Regiment. In 1879, the second son, Benjamin Parnell, was serving with the 22nd Bengal Native Infantry under Sir Samuel Browne VC (inventor of the Sam Browne belt) during the Second Afghan War, and later fought in the Sudan. His other brother, Charles, served with the 24th Regiment in the Ashanti Campaign, and was a favourite of Sir Garnet Wolseley.

Gonville Bromhead entered the 2nd Battalion, 24th Regiment as an ensign by purchase in April 1867, where he was always helpful to new recruits. He became a champion at boxing, wrestling and singlestick. He was promoted to lieutenant in October 1871 by selection, having made a good impression with his fellow officers. However, he started to develop a serious hearing problem, but contrary to popular belief this did not affect his ability to command his men (deafness in the army at this time was not uncommon; Sir Evelyn Wood VC went deaf as a young ensign during the Crimean War but continued to command in the field for many years).

In February 1878, Bromhead's battalion was dispatched to the Cape Colony to assist in the Ninth Xhosa War (aka the Ninth Cape Frontier War). B Company took part in several offensive operations at the conclusion of the war. During an assault on a Xhosa position in May, the company's commander, Caption A.G. Godwin-Austen, was wounded accidentally by one of his own men, and command of the company temporarily passed to Bromhead. In August the battalion was sent to Pietermaritzburg to prepare for the upcoming Zulu war, arriving at Rorke's Drift on 9 January 1879, where the army had commandeered Otto Witt's mission station for a supply depot.

At approximately 3.00 pm, the news of the disaster at iSandlwana came in while Bromhead and Commissary Dunne were relaxing with their pipes near the tents. Bromhead sent a man to report the news to Lieutenant Chard, who was working with the ponts at the river, while he, Dunne, Acting Commissary James Dalton and Surgeon James Reynolds, who had just come back from the Oscarberg hill, decided that with barricades placed around the position they had a fair chance of making a stand. Bromhead sent six men – 801 Cole, Hook, 716 Jones, 593 Jones, 1395 Williams and 1398 Williams – to help defend the patients and hospital building. Some of the patients were also armed to help with the defence. On his arrival at the post Chard asked Bromhead to station the men at the almost finished ramparts.

After the initial attack against the south wall, the Zulus moved around to the north-west and threw themselves at the incomplete barricades in front of the hospital, making some very determined attacks, eventually pushing the soldiers back. The Zulus poured over the defences and on seeing the danger, Bromhead led a bayonet charge that forced the enemy back out of the perimeter and into cover, from where they made continued attacks. Six times they broke in, and six times Bromhead led counter-attacks to throw them out, until it became hopeless and they were ordered to withdraw to the inner defence, leaving the hospital almost surrounded.

Bromhead was stationed behind the biscuit boxes where they met the north wall when a Zulu who had got over the barricade was about to stab him from behind. Seeing this, Private Hitch came to his rescue and killed the warrior. Later, Hitch was hit by a bullet, shattering his right shoulder, and Bromhead now came to his aid, shooting a Zulu, and secured Hitch's arm with his own waist belt. Bromhead gave him his revolver to use and continued the fight with a rifle. When the redoubt in front of the storehouse was completed, Bromhead joined Chard, giving orders and warning the men not to waste ammunition. In the morning, after the garrison had been relieved, Bromhead and Chard found a bottle of beer and together drank to their survival.

For his part in the defence, Bromhead was mentioned in despatches, and was awarded the Victoria Cross, gazetted on 2 May 1879. He was promoted to captain and brevet major, dated 23 January 1879, and was mentioned in despatches again on 1 and 15 March, before being presented with his VC by Lord Wolseley at Utrecht on 22 August 1897. Both he and Chard were mentioned in the House of Commons.

In September 1879, Bromhead sailed with his battalion on the troopship *Himalaya* to Gibraltar. While on leave in England in 1880, he had an audience with Queen Victoria, who gave him a signed portrait of herself. In June he was invited to the Lincoln Masonic Hall, where the mayor presented him with a jewelled dress sword and an illuminated address. During an acceptance speech while guest of honour at a banquet at the Assembly Room he acknowledged Chard, Reynolds and Dalton's parts in the defence. He was also given a revolver by the tenants of Thurlby Hall, Lincolnshire, the ancestral home of the Bromhead baronets.

August 1880 saw Bromhead posted to the East Indies, where he remained until March 1882, returning to England in the summer and attending the Hythe School of Musketry, gaining a First Class Extra

Certificate. In January 1882 he embarked on HMS *Serapis* to join his battalion at Secunderabad, India. He took part in the expedition to Upper Burma from October 1886 to May 1888.

Gonville Bromhead died on 9 February 1891 from typhoid fever, while on active service at Camp Dabhaura, Allahabad, India. He is buried in the New Cantonment Cemetery, Plot B1, Grave 66. He left his medals to his brother Charles and the rest of his estate to his sisters Alice Margaret and Elizabeth Frances. His VC is held by the Regimental Museum of the Royal Welsh, Brecon, Powys.

William 'Wilson' ALLAN (ALLEN), Rorke's Drift, 22/23 January 1879

William Allan (spelt Allen on his recruiting documents) was born in 1843 in Kyloe, near Berwick-upon-Tweed, Northumberland. He enlisted at York on 27 October 1859, joining the 2nd Battalion, 24th Regiment at Aldershot four days later. Private Allan served on the sugar island of Mauritius in the Indian Ocean and was confined to the cells on a number of occasions in the early 1860s. After thirteen years in the East, in April 1874 he returned to the depot at Brecon. In 1876 he married Sara-Ann Reeves, she being fifteen years younger. Allan was promoted to lance corporal in May 1876 and full corporal in July 1877.

William Allan.

Posted to the 2nd Battalion of the 24th Foot in January 1878, he sailed to South Africa and took part in the Ninth Xhosa War (aka the Ninth Cape Frontier War). Allan was promoted to lance sergeant in May 1878 but he reduced to corporal in October while at Pietermaritzburg for being drunk on duty.

On 22 January 1879, Corporal Allan was one of a number of sharpshooters posted to the south wall, facing the Oskarberg hill at

Rorke's Drift, where two wagons had been included in the barricade. The Zulus advanced to within fifty paces before devastating rifle fire stopped them. Later, when the hospital was being evacuated and the Zulus were climbing over the barricade to get at the patients, Corporal Allan and Private Hitch kept communications open between the hospital and the inner defence while the patients were moved to safety. The area was being swept by Zulu fire and Allan was hit in the shoulder. Surgeon Reynolds attended to his wounds, but Allan was unable to carry on the fight. He assisted in handing out ammunition to the men throughout the night.

Allan's grave, Monmouth Cemetery.

For his conduct he was mentioned in despatches and awarded the VC, gazetted on 2 May 1879. After being moved to Helpmekaar, he wrote home saying, 'My arm is mending quickly.' Allan sailed home on board the *Tamar* and was taken to the Netley Military Hospital in Hampshire. His arm was left partly disabled but he was fit enough the join the South Wales Borderers Militia in November. On 9 December 1879, he and four other men were presented with their VCs by the Queen at Windsor Castle.

William Allan was appointed Provisional Sergeant at Colchester depot in June 1880. In 1886 he was appointed Sergeant Instructor of Musketry to 4th Volunteer Battalion, South Wales Borderers at Monmouth. In February 1890, Allan fell victim to influenza and was ill for weeks before dying on 12 March. He was buried with full military honours at Monmouth Cemetery, Section B, Grave 25. After the death of his wife, Allan's VC was purchased by Philip Wilkins, and is now held by the Regimental Museum of the Royal Welsh, Brecon, Powys.

Frederick HITCH, Rorke's Drift, 22/23 January 1879

Frederick Hitch was born on 29 November 1856 in Southgate, Edmonton, Middlesex, the son of John and Sara Hitch. His father was employed as a shoemaker. Before enlisting into the 24th Foot on 7 March 1877, Hitch worked as a labourer. Sent to South Africa with his regiment, he took part in the last of the Xhosa Wars (aka the Ninth Cape Frontier War).

On the afternoon of 22 January, Hitch was brewing tea for the company when Lieutenant Bromhead told him to get onto the store roof to look out for the approaching Zulus. Hitch observed the advance of the enemy, estimating their

Frederick Hitch.

number at over 4,000. Coming back down, he took up position between the hospital and the storehouse to meet the first Zulu assault. He shot at least one Zulu before another managed to seize the muzzle of his rifle, but he was able to load and shoot this warrior too.

At about 7.00 pm, Hitch took up position in the compound with Corporal Allan. They kept the enemy at bay while the hospital patients were evacuated and taken to the inner defence. During the next Zulu assault Hitch killed a warrior who was about to stab Bromhead from behind, and then was shot himself at close range by another warrior, shattering his right shoulder. Bromhead now came to his aid, and after securing Hitch's arm with his own waist belt, Bromhead gave him his revolver to use (Bromhead by this time was using a rifle). Hitch was in great pain but was also able to help hand out ammunition to the men throughout the night.

Next morning, Hitch was seen by Surgeon Reynolds, who removed thirty-nine pieces of bone fragment from his shoulder. For his part in the defence Hitch was mentioned in despatches, and awarded the Victoria Cross, gazetted on 2 May 1879. Allan and Hitch travelled back home together and both went to the Netley Hospital in Hampshire, where Hitch gave an account of his part in the battle to the press. Queen

Victoria visited the hospital on 12 August and presented Hitch with his medal. Hitch was discharged from the army on 25 August 1879 due to his shoulder wound.

On his return to London, Hitch was employed by the Corps of Commissionaires. In July 1880 he married Emma Matilda Maurice; they had eleven children together, three of whom died in infancy. While Hitch was working at the Royal United Services Institute, Cecil Rhodes visited him to congratulate him on his award. In February of 1901, his VC was stolen from him while he was in hospital after falling from a ladder. Forced to pay for a replacement himself, he soon lost his job when he was accused of faking the theft to cover up that he had sold the medal, although this was never proved.

In 1901 he went to work as a horse-drawn hansom cab driver, later using a motor car. One of his fellow drivers was Joseph Farmer VC, who was awarded his medal for action in 1881 (see Chapter 6), and they became great friends. After the death of his wife, Hitch lived alone in Cranbrook Road, Chiswick. During Christmas of 1912, the taxi drivers at his depot went on strike. Being in good health, he visited friends in Epsom, but on the morning of 6 January 1913, he complained of pains in his side and he died later the same day. The inquest found he had died of pleuropneumonia and heart failure.

Frederick Hitch was buried with full military honours by the South Wales Borderers in Chiswick Old Cemetery, Block P, Grave 17. Among the mourners were John Fielding VC, Frank Bourne DCM and Joseph Farmer VC, as well as many of Hitch's fellow cabbies. His very impressive headstone (more of a monument in reality) was paid for by public subscription, one of the donations coming from Colonel John Chard's family. Hitch's VC was purchased on behalf of the South Wales Borderers in 1929 and is now held by the Regimental Museum of the Royal Welsh, Brecon, Powys.

Hitch's grave, Chiswick Old Cemetery, West London.

Alfred Henry 'Harry' HOOK, Rorke's Drift, 22/23 January 1879

Harry Hook was born on 6 August 1850 in Churcham, Gloucestershire, the oldest of six children of Henry and Ellen Hook. His father was a labourer and the family lived in a house called 'Birdwood', also known locally as 'Hook's Farm'. In around 1871 the family moved to Monmouth, although Harry went to live and work in the village of Huntly as a rural labourer.

In May 1869 Hook enlisted in the Royal Monmouthshire Militia. His service in the Militia lasted until May 1874, and in March 1877 he entered the 24th Regiment of Foot at Monmouth, signing on for six years. His reason for enlisting may have had something to do with him having problems paying off the mortgage on a property at Huntley. Hook was posted to the 2nd Battalion, becoming 1373 Private Alfred Hook, and was posted to Dover Citadel, where he met Fred Hitch, before transferring to Chatham. Hook sailed to South Africa with his battalion and saw service in the Ninth Xhosa War (aka the Ninth Cape Frontier War) in 1878.

Harry Hook.

On the afternoon of 22 January 1879, Hook's B Company was stationed at Rorke's Drift, where he was assigned as cook for the hospital patients. Along with five other men, he was ordered to defend the hospital, where some of the patients were also being armed. Hook was posted in a small room in the south-west corner with Private Thomas Cole and a native, but as the fighting started, Cole left to man the barricade outside in front of the hospital. There was a door leading to another room in which there were eight patients, and another leading out of the building, which was barricaded. There was also a window.

The initial Zulu attack was launched against the barricade between the hospital and the storehouse; men from both buildings were able to give fire support but the Zulus soon moved their attention towards the hospital. Hook shot several warriors through the window as the Zulus closed in and assaulted the building. As the hospital roof started to burn and Hook was now alone with the native, he was forced to abandon the room and the native, whom he could not persuade to leave with him.

He now found himself in charge of nine men, and was soon joined by Private John Williams (Fielding), who had rescued a patient from another room. They worked together, Hook keeping the Zulus at bay while Williams smashed through the far wall. The Zulus were trying to grab Hook's rifle and bayonet, when an assegai thrust wounded him on the scalp. When the hole in the wall was big enough, Williams got all the patients out except for Private John Connolly, who was suffering from an injured knee. Hook saw his chance and rushed from the doorway, dragging Connolly through the hole before the Zulus could rush in. Hook now defended this room, fighting at the hole made by Williams to stop the Zulus pursuing, shooting and bayoneting many while Williams made another hole in the far wall. Again, Williams helped the patients through to the next room while Hook held the Zulus back, and once more, Hook helped Connolly through the hole. The last room had been defended by Privates Robert Jones and William Jones, who had by now escaped through a widow into the inner defence perimeter. Hook and Williams followed them with the patients and took up positions in the inner defence.

As the night wore on many men became parched with thirst and were in need of water, but the water cart had been abandoned near the hospital building. Hook and two other men decided to risk retrieving the cart.

After daylight on the 23rd, when the Zulus had withdrawn, Hook was sent out to collect weapons. He was walking by a dry watercourse carrying assegais when he saw a Zulu lying on the ground with a leg wound. As he passed him, the warrior sprang forward and grabbed Hook's rifle butt, trying to pull him to the ground. Hook dropped the spears and shot his assailant.

Hook had returned to his duties as hospital cook when the relief column arrived, and he was ordered to report to Lieutenant Bromhead, who took him to Lord Chelmsford. Thus, Hook found himself standing before Lord Chelmsford in his shirtsleeves (his tunic had been destroyed in the hospital fire), with his braces hanging down, answering questions about his part in the fight for the hospital. As a professional soldier, Hook wanted to get another tunic but was told there was no time, and he was not happy at being presented to His Lordship in such a manner.

For his bravery at Rorke's Drift Hook was mentioned in despatches and awarded the Victoria Cross, gazetted on 2 May 1879. On 29 January 1879, he was transferred to G Company as orderly to Major Black. Hook accompanied him on a visit to iSandlwana, where he picked up a bible from the battlefield, and this is now on display at the regimental museum. Hook remained stationed at Rorke's Drift for the rest of the campaign, and on 3 August 1879 was presented with his VC by Lord Wolseley at the location where he had earned it. He is one of the very few men to be so awarded at the location of the deed.

In September 1879 Hook sailed to Gibraltar. He was entitled to a penny a day good conduct pay but decided to buy his discharge for £18, leaving the army at Brecon in June 1880. On his return to Huntley it is thought he found that his common law wife had sold his property and remarried, believing he had been killed in action. When his father died that year, Hook moved to London.

In September 1881, he applied for a job at the British Museum, and after being recommended by Major Bromhead and Lord Chelmsford, was taken on in December as an 'inside book duster'. In April 1882 he was appointed as umbrella caretaker in the Reading Room at the museum, a position he held until his retirement in 1904.

Hook became a member of the Loyal St James Lodge of Oddfellows; he served as a corporal in the Bloomsbury Rifle Volunteer Club, and was Sergeant Instructor of Musketry in the 1st Volunteer Battalion, Royal Fusiliers, serving with them for twenty years. A silver-plated memorial trophy bearing his name was presented to the British Museum Rifle Association and is awarded for services to the association.

In the 1890s Hook moved to Pimlico, where he met Ada Taylor, and on 10 April 1897 they were married at St Andrew's Church, Islington. They had two girls, Victoria Catherine (VC), born in 1899, and Letitia Jean, born 1902.

Hook was advised to return to Gloucestershire in 1904 due to poor health, so in December of that year he resigned from his job. The museum trustees granted him a pension of £40 6s 11d per year. He was placed in the care of Phoenix Lodge of Oddfellows at Gloucester, who recommended him to a doctor. His family moved into No. 2 Osborn Villas, Rosebury Avenue, Gloucester.

Rorke's Drift   23

Hook's grave, Churcham, Gloucestershire.

Harry Hook died on 12 March 1905 from pulmonary tuberculosis, aged 54. His funeral took place six days later, attended by thousands of people; twenty-three regiments were also represented. He was buried with full military honours by the South Wales Borderers in St Andrew's churchyard, Churcham. Ade received a letter of sympathy from John Williams (Fielding) VC and Frederick Hitch VC attended the funeral with his son, who as a corporal in the South Wales Borderers was a pall bearer.

In September 1906 Ada and her daughters attended Harry's graveside when Colonel Curll of the South Wales Borderers unveiled a memorial cross on the grave, inscribed: 'Erected by admiring civilians and local regiments, in memory of his heroic share in the defence of Rorke's Drift, Natal, 1879.' Ade died in 1929. Harry Hook's VC is held by the Regimental Museum of the Royal Welsh, Brecon, Powys.

Robert JONES, Rorke's Drift, 22/23 January 1879

Robert Jones was born on 19 August 1857 in Penrhos, near Raglan, Monmouthshire. He was the son of a farm worker, a job he also took up before enlisting into the 24th Foot in January 1876 – a decision his father was unhappy with. Jones was posted to the 2nd Battalion on 28 January at Dover Citadel, becoming 716 Private Robert Jones. He sailed for service in the Ninth Cape Frontier War, and later found himself at Rorke's Drift.

On the afternoon of 22 January 1879, Private Robert Jones was posted to a room with Private William Jones and a number of patients. The room faced the Oskarberg hill and had one window and a door opening to the outside and an internal door. The Joneses fought off the Zulus until their ammunition ran out and the warriors closed in. Fighting was now hand-to-hand, bayonet to assegai, during which Robert Jones was wounded three times. But the two Joneses managed to get all but one of the patients out and into the next room. Robert Jones tried to go back for Sergeant Robert Maxfield, who was delirious, but was only in time to see him being killed by the pursuing warriors. The building was by now ablaze and the Joneses, with the patients who were able to join the inner defence, running a gauntlet of Zulu fire as they crossed the compound.

Robert Jones.

For his part in the fight for the hospital, Robert Jones was mentioned in despatches and awarded the Victoria Cross, gazetted on 2 May 1879. He was presented with his medal at the same time as Private Wassall, on 11 September 1879, by Lord Wolseley at Utrecht.

Jones went on to serve in Gibraltar and India, returning to Britain in November 1881. He was transferred to the Army Reserve, being recalled in August 1882, but was finally discharged from the Reserve in January 1888.

Jones worked as a farm labourer and in 1885 married Elizabeth Hopkins; they had one son and four daughters. He gained employment as a groundsman for Major de la Hay at Crossways House, Peterchurch, Herefordshire.

Jones suffered from pains in the head and reoccurring nightmares about Zulus. In August 1898 he collapsed, and although he recovered, his wife noticed a change in his character. On 6 September 1898 she noticed him behaving strangely before setting off for work. He took his employer's shotgun to go hunting. Shortly after, a shot was heard and Jones was found dead, with the back of his head blown away. An inquest found that he had committed suicide while of unsound mind. He was buried on 8 September in St Peter's churchyard in Hereford.

Some, including his family, have tried to have the verdict overturned on the grounds that the shotgun was known to have a hair trigger and Jones had tripped while climbing over a wall. However, it would seem unlikely that an experienced soldier would climb a wall with a loaded shotgun which he knew had a hair trigger. It would also be difficult for the barrel to end up in his mouth by accident. Jones's VC is now in the Ashcroft Gallery at the Imperial War Museum, London.

Robert Jones's grave, St Peter's churchyard, Hereford.

William JONES, Rorke's Drift, 22/23 January 1879

Jones was born (possibly on 16 August) 1839 in Bristol, the son of James Jones, a building labourer. Jones enlisted into the 24th Foot in December 1858 after being attested. It is unclear whether his attest had anything to do with his enlistment. He was promoted to corporal in September 1859, while at Mauritius, East Africa, but was reduced to private in September 1860. Jones also served in Burma and India. While back in Wales he married Elizabeth Goddard.

Jones sailed to South Africa, taking his wife with him. It is believed she

William Jones.

was taken ill during childbirth, as it was reported on 18 June 1879 in the *Natal Mercury* newspaper: 'When he came here with his regiment his wife came with him, but after some time, she became dangerously ill, and he obtained leave of absence to come down to attend to her.' Jones rented a room and by working day and night earned money to care for her until she died. She was buried the next day and Jones left to rejoin his regiment. The child seems to have survived as it is believed his son, also named William, was sent to Wales into the care of relatives.

On the afternoon of 22 January 1879, Jones was one of six men assigned to defend the hospital at Rorke's Drift, being posted to a room with Robert Jones and a number of hospital patients. The room faced the Oskarberg hill and had one window and a door opening to the outside and an internal door. The Joneses fought off the Zulus until their ammunition ran out and the warriors closed in. Fighting was now hand-to-hand, bayonet to assegai, but the two Joneses managed to get all but one of the patients out and into the next room. Robert Jones tried to go back for Sergeant Maxfield, who was delirious, but was only in time to see him being killed by the pursuing warriors. The building was by now ablaze and the Joneses, with the patients who were able to join the inner defence, running a gauntlet of Zulu fire as they crossed the compound. William Jones fought through the remainder of the night on the inner perimeter.

For his part in the defence Jones was mentioned in despatches and awarded the Victoria Cross, gazetted on 2 May 1879. In September, Jones was examined by a medical panel and found to be suffering from chronic rheumatism of the joints, and was invalided to the Netley Military Hospital in Hampshire. On 13 January 1880, he was invited to Windsor Castle and was presented his VC by Queen Victoria. He was discharged from service in February 1880.

While in Manchester, Jones lived with Elizabeth Frodsham, a widow with five children, and they had two further children together. In the 1880s he appeared on stage to recite an account of the Battle of Rorke's Drift action, and in 1887–88 he toured with American showman Buffalo Bill Cody (himself a recipient of the Medal of Honor) in his Wild West Show. In 1893, having hit hard times, Jones was forced to pawn his VC for £5, eventually having to give up the pawn ticket. At 61 years of age he married Elizabeth.

In 1898, a fraudulent attempt to claim an official VC in William Jones's name was made in Adelaide, Australia. The medal turned up in Preston, Lancashire, in 1917. Suffering from poor health, Jones was mostly confined to home. Sometimes he would have nightmares and leave the house, once taking his granddaughter with him. In 1912 he was found wandering the streets, and although able to identify himself could give no address so was taken to the workhouse in Salford, from where his wife had to collect him.

William Jones died on 15 April 1913 at the house of his daughter, Emily Goodwin, in Ardwick, Manchester. Six days later, a large crowd watched as his funeral cortège made its way to Philips Park Cemetery, C of E Common Ground, Section D-887, Briscoe Lane, Manchester. The helmet he wore at Rorke's Drift was placed on his coffin. Jones was buried with full military honours by the South Wales Borderers. His VC is held by the Regimental Museum of the Royal Welsh, Brecon, Powys.

William Jones's grave, Philips Park Cemetery, Manchester.

John WILLIAMS (born FIELDING), Rorke's Drift, 22/23 January 1879

John Fielding was born on 24 May 1857 in Abergavenny, Monmouthshire, one of ten children of Michael and Margaret Fielding. John's father was employed as a gardener. When John was 5 years old the family moved to Cwmbran as his father was in search of work. John was first employed as a labourer at the age of 7, by the Patent Nut and Bolt Company, which had factory in Cwmbran. His first taste of military service came when he joined the Royal Monmouthshire Militia in February 1877. It is not really clear why John Fielding enlisted under the name John Williams. It would seem mostly likely that he was in dispute with his father, possibly because he was against him joining up. He enlisted into the 24th

Regiment of Foot on 22 May 1877 (the same day as Joseph Williams), becoming 1395 Private John Williams, both men being posted to 2nd Battalion at Dover Citadel. Williams sailed to South Africa in February 1878 for service in the last of the Xhosa Wars (aka the Ninth Cape Frontier War).

On the afternoon of 22 January 1879 at Rorke's Drift, John Williams and Private Joseph Williams, along with patients including Private John Horrigan (who was well enough to help with the defence) and two who were bedridden,

John Williams.

were stationed in a distant corner of the hospital. The only door in the room led out of the building. The three men were firing through loopholes made in the walls, and were able to hold the Zulus at bay for an hour, until their ammunition ran low, enabling the Zulus to close in and smash the flimsy door. The men were now trapped; John Williams began to dig at the partition wall with his bayonet, while Horrigan and Joseph Williams held back the warriors as they tried to force their way in.

Joseph Williams had the bayonet wrenched from his rifle and the Zulus smashed open the door, dragging him and two patients out and subsequently killing them all. By this time John Williams had made a hole big enough to get into the next room. With the help of Horrigan they were able to take a patient through to the next room, but Horrigan was killed by the pursuing warriors. Joining Private Alfred 'Harry' Hook in another room, both men now worked together, Hook keeping the Zulus at bay while Williams cut his way into the next room, and they fought their way out of the building, bringing eight patients with them to the inner defence. It is said that Williams's hair turned white due to the harrowing experience of the battle.

For his conduct in the battle for the hospital, John Williams was mentioned in despatches and awarded the Victoria Cross, gazetted on 2 May 1879. After the Zulu War he was posted to Gibraltar, where, on 1 March 1880, he was presented with his VC by Major General Anderson.

In August 1880, Williams sailed with his battalion to India, reaching Bombay on 1 September, and was at once sent to Poonah. But Lord Roberts had already relieved Kandahar and inflicted a decisive defeat on the Afghans, so the 2nd Battalion was diverted to Secunderabad, arriving on 16 September, where Williams ended his service. In October 1883, he returned to Wales and married Elizabeth Murphy, and transferred to the Army Reserve, becoming a sergeant in the 3rd Battalion, South Wales Borderers. Williams was discharged in May 1893, and was attached to the civilian staff at Brecon barracks until his retirement on 20 May 1920.

He was appointed Recruiting Officer at Brecon during the First World War, where he received the news that his oldest son, Tom, had been killed in action while serving with the South Wales Borderers during the retreat from Mons.

Williams attended the garden party hosted on 26 June 1920 by King George V and Queen Mary at Buckingham Palace, and was present at a VC dinner held in the House of Lords by the Prince of Wales on 9 November 1929.

After his wife died John Williams went to live with his widowed daughter, Margaret, at Ty Coch, Cwmbran. On 24 November 1932, John Williams took his daily walk to the home of his other daughter, Catherine. While there he became ill and died from heart failure in the early hours of the 25th. His coffin lay in state at Wesley Street Catholic Church, and his funeral cortège, half a mile long, was filmed by Pathé News. There was a place of honour for Zulu War veterans, and floral tributes came from the families of Frederick Hitch VC and Henry Hook VC. His close friend, John H. Williams VC, DCM, MM, attended as a representative of Ebbw Vale Royal British Legion. The last surviving Zulu War VC was buried with full military honours by the

John Williams's (Fielding) grave, St Michael's churchyard, Llanfihangel, Llantarnam, Gwent.

South Wales Borderers, who later erected a memorial stone at his grave in St Michael's churchyard, Llanfihangel, Llantarnam, Gwent. His VC is held by the Regimental Museum of the Royal Welsh, Brecon, Powys.

James Henry REYNOLDS, Rorke's Drift, 22/23 January 1879

James Reynolds.

James Reynolds was born on 3 February 1844 in Kingstown (now Dún Laoghaire), County Dublin, the son of Laurence Reynolds JP, of Dalyston House, Granard, County Longford, Ireland. Educated at Castle Knock School, Reynolds obtained his Bachelor of Medicine and Bachelor of Surgery from Trinity College, Dublin, before joining the Army Medicinal Department in March 1867.

In 1869 he transferred to the 36th Regiment of Foot as their medical officer. He received a commendation from the C-in-C, Lord Sandhurst, for his efficient service during a cholera outbreak while with the regiment in India in 1869–70, after which he was invalided home. Reynolds became a surgeon on 1 March 1873, and sailed to Africa with the 1st Battalion, 24th Foot, taking part in the Griqualand West campaign of 1875 and the last of the Xhosa Wars (aka the Ninth Cape Frontier War) in 1877–78, being present at the action around Impetu, where the 24th was besieged for several weeks until January 1878.

Surgeon Reynolds was at Rorke's Drift on the afternoon of 24 January 1879; at about 12.30 pm, the thud of heavy guns could be heard in the direction of iSandlwana. Reynolds, with Otto Witt and Reverend Smith, decided to go up the Oscarberg hill. The following account is in Reynolds's own words:

> At 1.30 pm a large body of natives marched over the slope of iSandlwana in our direction, their purpose evidently being to examine ravines and ruined kraals for hiding fugitives. These men we took to

be our native contingent. Soon afterwards appeared four horsemen on the Natal side of the river galloping in the direction of our post, one of them was a regular soldier, and feeling they might possibly be messengers for additional medical assistance, I hurried down to the hospital as they rode up. They looked awfully scared, and I was at once startled to find one of them was riding Surgeon Major Shephard's pony. They shouted frantically, 'The camp at iSandlwana has been taken by the enemy and all our men in it massacred, [and] that no power could stand against the enormous number of the Zulus, and the only chance for us was in immediate flight.' Lieutenant Bromhead, Acting Commissary Dalton, and myself [Commissary Dunne was also present] forthwith consulted together, Lieutenant Chard not having as yet joined us from the pontoon, and we quickly decided that with barricades well placed around our present position a stand could best be made where we were. Just at this point Mr. Dalton's energies were invaluable. Without the smallest delay, he called upon his men to carry the mealie sacks here and there for the defences. Lieutenant Chard (RE) arrived as this work was in progress, and gave many useful orders as regards the lines of defence. He approved also of the hospital being taken in [to the defence perimeter], and between the hospital orderlies, convalescent patients (eight or ten) and myself, we loopholed the building and made a continuation of the commissariat defences around it. The hospital, however, occupied a wretched position, having a garden and shrubbery close by, which afterwards proved so favourable to the enemy; but comparing our prospects with that of the iSandlwana affair, we felt that the mealie barriers might afford us a moderately fair chance.

At about 3:30 the enemy made their first appearance in a large crowd on the hospital side of our post, coming on in skirmishing order at a slow slinging run. We opened fire on them from the hospital at 600 yards, and although the bullets ploughed through their midst and knocked over many, there was no check or alteration made in their approach. As they got nearer they became more scattered, but the bulk of them rushed for the hospital and the garden in front of it.

We found ourselves quickly surrounded by the enemy with their strong force holding the garden and shrubbery. From all sides but especially the latter places, they poured on us a continuous fire, to which our men replied as quickly as they could reload their rifles. Again and again the Zulus pressed forward and retreated, until at last they forced themselves so daringly, and in such numbers, as to climb over the mealie sacks in front of the hospital, and drove the defenders from there behind an entrenchment of biscuit boxes, hastily formed with much judgement and forethought by Lieutenant Chard. A heavy fire from behind it was resumed with renewed confidence, and with little confusion or delay, checking successfully the natives, and permitting a semi flank fire from another part of the laager to play on them destructively. At this time too, the loopholes in the hospital were made great use of. It was, however, only temporary, as, after a short respite, they came on again with renewed vigour. Some of them gained the hospital verandah, and there got hand to hand with our men defending the doors. Once they were driven back from there, but others soon pressed forward in their stead, and having occupied the verandah in larger numbers than before, pushed their way right into the hospital, where confusion on our side naturally followed. Everyone tried to escape as best they could, and owing to the rooms not communicating with one another, the difficulties were insurmountable. Private Hook, 2/24th Regiment, who was acting as hospital cook, and Private Connolly, 2/24th Regiment, a patient in hospital, made their way into the open at the back of the hospital by breaking a hole in the wall. Most of the patients escaped through a small window looking into what may be styled the neutral ground. Those who madly tried to get off by leaving the front of the hospital were killed with the exception of Gunner Howard.

The only men actually killed in the hospital were three, excluding a Kaffir under treatment for compound fracture of the femur. The names were Sergeant Maxfield, Private Jenkins, both unable to assist in their escape, being debilitated by fever, and Private Adams, who was well able to move about, but could not be persuaded to leave his temporary refuge in a small room. The engagement continued more or less until 7 o'clock p.m. and then, when we were beginning to consider our situation as rather hopeless, the fire from our opponents appreciably slackened giving us some time for reflection. Lieutenant Chard here again shined in resource. Anticipating the Zulus making one more united dash for the fort, and possibly gaining entrance, he converted an immense stack of mealies standing in the middle of our enclosure, and originally cone fashioned, into a comparatively safe place for a last retreat. Just as it was completed, smoke from the hospital appeared and shortly burst into flames. During the whole night following desultory fire was carried on by the enemy, and several feigned attacks were made, but nothing of a continued or determined effort was again attempted by them. About 6 o'clock a.m., we found, after careful reconnoitring, that all the Zulus with the exception of a couple of stragglers had left our immediate vicinity, and soon afterwards a large body of men were seen at a distance marching towards us.

Reynolds's account is interesting in a number of ways; his times are a little different to most other sources, and he does not even mention that he carried ammunition to the men in the hospital, sometimes going outside of the perimeter, during which his helmet was struck by a bullet. He seems to have underestimated the numbers killed in the hospital fighting, and he does not mention the final Zulu attack, which is odd as he was placed in the final redoubt with the wounded during it.

Reynolds was mentioned in despatches and was promoted to surgeon major, dated 23 January 1879. But it was June before his VC was gazetted, and only then after it was mooted that it was not only the Imperial soldiers who should have been awarded the VC for this action (the eight Imperial soldiers' VCs were gazetted on 2 May). Reynolds stayed at Rorke's Drift, tending to the wounded, and was present at the Battle of Ulundi on 4 July. Lord Wolseley presented him with his VC at St Paul's church in KwaZulu Natal, South Africa, on 16 July 1879. Reynolds sailed home on the troopship *Eagle*, arriving in October 1879.

Upon his return to Ireland he was appointed senior medical officer for the expedition to aid Captain Charles Boycott, during the so-called Irish Land

Reynolds's grave, St Mary's RC Cemetery, Kensal Rise, London.

War of 1880. Later that year, Reynolds married Elizabeth McCormick. He was promoted to lieutenant colonel on 1 April 1887 and brigade surgeon, lieutenant colonel on 25 December 1892. Reynolds retired from the army on 8 January 1896. In November 1929, he attended a VC dinner at the House of Lords, where he and John Williams (Fielding) VC were two of the guests of honour.

James Reynolds died on 4 March 1932 in the Empire Nursing Home, London. He was buried in St Mary's RC Cemetery, Grave RC-504, Harrow Road, Kensal Rise, London. His VC is on display at the Army Medical Services Museum, Mytchett, Surrey.

James Langley DALTON, Rorke's Drift, 22/23 January 1879

Born c.1833 in St Andrew's Parish, London, James Dalton enlisted into the 85th (Shropshire) Regiment of Foot in November 1849, giving his age as 17 years and 11 months, although it is generally believed he was younger. In 1853 he sailed on the troopship *Marion* for East Africa and service in Mauritius. He then sailed to South Africa to take part in the Eighth Cape Frontier War. Dalton returned to England and transferred to the Commissariat Corps in 1862 as a corporal. He was promoted to sergeant in January 1863 and colour sergeant in June of the same year. Dalton attended musketry school in 1864, and became a clerk and master sergeant in 1866.

James Dalton.

In 1868 he went to North America and served with Lord Wolseley during the Red River Expedition of 1870. While there, the Commissariat was reorganised and Dalton was transferred to the Army Service Corps. He returned to England in 1871 as a staff sergeant and was discharged from the army as a senior warrant officer after twenty-two years of service.

Back in South Africa by 1877, Dalton volunteered for service in the last of the Xhosa Wars (aka the Ninth Cape Frontier War). There being a need for trained staff, he was appointed acting commissary in December 1877, when he was in sole command of the Ibeka depot, serving the garrison of the 24th Regiment. The garrison was under constant threat and was at one time cut off by thousands of Gcaleka tribesmen. For his efficiency and energy in supplying three British columns he was mentioned in despatches by the GOC, the only civilian to be so.

At the end of 1878 Dalton volunteered for the upcoming Zulu War, riding through the pouring rain with Louis Byrne to join the troops at Helpmekaar. When he arrived at Rorke's Drift he helped to set up the commissary store there under Assistant Commissariat Dunne, who had also served in the Ninth Cape Frontier War.

When news of the disaster at iSandlwana came in, Dalton joined Commissary Dunne, Lieutenant Bromhead and Surgeon Reynolds to consider their options. It was most likely Dalton who first suggested they should make a defence with barricades, having remembered his experience at Ibeka. Once agreed he actively supervised the men with great vigour and much work was carried out due to his diligence. When Lieutenant Chard arrived he approved of the defensive measures being carried out and the hospital being taken into the defence perimeter. Dalton then instructed the colonial officers to rally the natives and stop them running off before the work was completed.

When the attack started Dalton took up a position by the hospital and his deadly fire did great work. He shot a Zulu who had seized the muzzle of Corporal Miller's rifle, and was in the act of stabbing him, thus saving his life. Dalton continually went along the barricade, exposing himself to enemy fire and cheering the men on. He seemed to hit a warrior with every shot he fired. When a Zulu ran up near the barricade, Dalton called out, 'Pot that fellow', while simultaneously shooting another Zulu, but at the same time he was hit by a bullet in the shoulder. He handed his rifle to Chard so calmly that he did not realise Dalton had been severely wounded. Reynolds came over and began to dress his wound. Chard took his remaining cartridges from his pockets and Dalton was placed by the pile of mealie bags in front of the storehouse, as Commissary Dunne built up a redoubt around him. Dalton continued to shout encouragement to the men, earning their respect, and Dunne (who was considered for the VC, but not awarded it) referred to him as 'Dalton the lionhearted'.

Dalton was so severely wounded that he went on sick leave for six months at Pietermaritzburg. When the 24th Foot marched into town in October, the men of B Company saw Dalton in the crowd and raised a cheer to him. Not among the initial awards of the VC, news of Dalton's bravery began to reach senior officials, his award finally being gazetted on 18 November 1879, and only then after it was mooted that it was not only the Imperial soldiers who should have been awarded the VC for this action (the eight Imperial soldiers' VCs were gazetted on 2 May). He received the medal from General High Clifford VC at a parade in Fort Napier on 16 January 1880.

In November 1879 Dalton returned to service with a permanent commission as sub-assistant commissary at Fort Napier, and in December of that year was promoted to assistant commissary and placed on half pay. He sailed home to England in February 1880. It is believed he served in the North East Africa campaigns as a volunteer in the 1880s before returning to South Africa. Engaged in the goldfields at Little Bess Mine, in the Transvaal, Dalton held 1,500 shares. Shortly before Christmas 1886, he went to stay with his old friend, ex-Sergeant John Sherwood Williams, in Port Elizabeth. On 7 January, he spent all day in bed and died during the night.

James Dalton is buried in Russell Road RC Cemetery, Plot E, Port Elizabeth, South Africa. His headstone was erected by his old comrade John Sherwood Williams and friends of Natal. Dalton's VC is held by the RLC Museum, Deepcut, Camberley, Surrey.

Christian Ferdinand (aka Friederich) SCHIESS, Rorke's Drift, 22/23 January 1879

Christian Schiess was born in Burgdorf, Switzerland, on 7 April 1856, the son of Niclaus and Anna Schiess. His father was a stonecutter and was known as Bernese Schiess. Ferdinand and his sister Anna-Marie were raised in an orphanage following the death of their parents. Schiess joined the French Army in 1870, taking part in the Franco-

Memorial plaque to 'Friederich' (Christian) Schiess at the Rorke's Drift Museum, Natal.

Prussian War. He served in the Armée de l'Est, which surrendered in the area of Pontarlier, close to the Swiss border. Schiess was among 87,000 men to cross the Franco-Swiss border at Les Verriéres and was interned for six weeks. Schiess sailed to South Africa on board HMS *Adele* in 1877 and found work as a labourer. Later he volunteered for the last of the Xhosa Wars (aka the Cape Frontier Wars), serving with distinction.

At the start of the Anglo-Zulu War the 22-year-old veteran soldier Schiess was made a corporal in the 2nd Battalion, 3rd Regiment of the Natal Native Contingent (NNC) by Colonel Durnford. Due to poor equipment, in particular boots, Schiess and a number of other NNC NCOs were suffering from severe blisters and were left at Rorke's Drift when their unit moved on with the main column.

On the afternoon of 22 January 1879, he was in the hospital when he heard news of the Zulu advance, and he decided to join his comrades on the barricades, most likely on the north wall somewhere in front of the building. During the early attacks a Zulu grabbed his bayonet but Schiess was able to keep hold of his weapon, killing a number of the enemy. He was shot in the same foot that was blistered, causing him much pain, but he refused to go to the surgeon. Later, when Chard ordered the men to retire to the inner defence line and the Zulus occupied the wall of mealie bags, which had been abandoned, he crept along the outer wall to dislodge a Zulu who was shooting from close range. The Zulu shot Schiess's hat off, but he jumped onto the wall and bayoneted him. Schiess returned to his side of the wall and shot another warrior. When another Zulu came up to the wall, Schiess sprang onto the barricade and bayoneted him, before returning to the inner defensive perimeter. Schiess displayed great gallantry throughout the remainder of the night despite suffering from his wounds.

For his conspicuous gallantry, Schiess was mentioned in despatches, but it would be December before his VC was gazetted, and only then after it was mooted that it was not only the Imperial soldiers who should have been awarded the VC for this action. He was the first man serving with the South African forces under British command to be awarded the Victoria Cross. When the NNC was disbanded he joined Lonsdale's Horse in January 1880. Schiess was presented with his medal by Lord Wolseley on 3 February 1880, but being rather modest about it he soon put it in his pocket. However, it was reported that he enjoyed being driven about the town in an open-top carriage for the rest of the day.

Schiess left Lonsdale's Horse and was employed in the telegraph office in Durban. However, by 1884 he was unemployed and had fallen on hard times. He had applied for government work in Natal, but by the end of the year he was found on the streets of Cape Town, suffering from exposure and malnutrition. The Royal Navy gave him food and offered him a free passage to England on HMS *Serapis*; Schiess accepted but became ill on board and died on 14 December 1884. He was buried at sea at approximately latitude south 1300; longitude west 7024 in the South Atlantic, off the coast of Angola. The only known memorial to him is at Rorke's Drift.

Despite his destitution, Christian Schiess never parted with his Victoria Cross, it being found on his person after his death and was brought to England. It was kept in a drawer at the War Office for many years until 1960, when it was taken to the Army Museum at Sandhurst. When the National Army Museum opened in Chelsea in 1971, Schiess's VC was put on display there (I was lucky enough to hold his medal when I was volunteering there). Sadly, after the museum's recent renovation, it is no longer on display. There are no known photos of Schiess, but at the time of the Rorke's Drift action he was described as a short, stocky man, with a beard and an earring.

Chapter 3

Intombe River

Anthony Clarke BOOTH, Intombe River, 12 March 1879

Anthony Booth was born on 21 April 1846 in Carrington, Nottinghamshire. Very little is known of his early life prior to him enlisting into the 80th Regiment of Foot (later the South Staffordshire Regiment) in October 1864. He was promoted to corporal in July the following year but confined to the cells in September, after which he was reduced to private. Booth married Lucy O'Brien in September 1866, and was promoted to corporal again in April 1869.

He became a sergeant in 1872 and was posted to Malaya with a detachment of his regiment. He arrived at Singapore in March that year, and took part in an expedition to Perak to deal with a local uprising. His unit was responsible for capturing a stockade at Rassa.

Anthony Booth.

While en route to Mauritius Booth's detachment was diverted to South Africa, arriving in March 1877. Stationed at Pietermaritzburg until June 1878, the regiment was attached to Colonel Rowlands' column for an expedition against Chief Sekhukhune and the Pedi tribe. However, due to a serious drought, the expedition was called off. Rowlands' men now moved to the border with Zululand for the upcoming war against Cetshwayo.

After the disaster at iSandlwana, the 80th Regiment came under the command of Sir Evelyn Wood VC, who moved his force to Khambula, sending a detachment of the 80th commanded by Major Charles Tucker to garrison Lüneburg. The garrison was supplied by wagon and

Booth spent much of his time with the convoys. In March 1879 he was accompanying a convoy from Derby when the wagons became bogged down at the Intombe (or Ntombe) River.

On 7 March, Captain David Moriarty rode out with a company of the 80th and found the wagons scattered along the track north of the river. The wagons were collected together at Myer's Drift. Booth supervised the building of a raft and by the evening of the 11th had got two wagons across. The wagons on the north bank had been moved into a 'V' for protection but there were gaps between them. Captain Moriarty had been informed of this but nothing was done.

At about 4.45 am the next morning the camp on the north bank was attacked by a large Zulu force, the camp being overrun and many men, including Moriarty, were killed. On the south bank, Lieutenant Henry Harward ordered Booth to open fire and to fall back to a burnt-out mission station 400 metres to their rear. Harward then rode off in the direction of Lüneburg. Booth, seeing that some men from the north bank were being pursued by Zulus as they were trying to cross the river, went forward with a section of men to cover their retreat. Keeping up a steady fire the men were able to get across and Booth ordered them to make for the mission station as his small band of men covered them. Had it not been for Booth, not one man would have escaped.

On reaching Lüneburg, Harward reported to Major Tucker, who immediately hurried to the scene with reinforcements. On reaching the station they found that the Zulus had already retired. The next day Booth was promoted to colour sergeant.

The 80th joined Wood's Flying Column in April 1879 and Booth took part in the Battle of Ulundi on 4 July. Lord Wolseley ordered a parade in which the drivers that Booth saved at the Intombe River presented him with a belt and ammunition pouch, a knife, and a nickel silver revolver. For his action on 12 March, Booth was mentioned in despatches and his VC was gazetted on 23 February 1880. The delay was due to Harward being court-martialled for cowardice; he was found not guilty but resigned his commission shortly afterwards.

Anthony Booth was presented his VC by the Queen at Windsor Castle on 26 June 1880. He remained in the army until April 1884 and retired to Staffordshire. He died from jaundice on 8 December 1899 and is buried in St Michael's RC churchyard, Brierley Hill, Staffordshire. His VC is held by the Staffordshire Regiment Museum, Lichfield.

Chapter 4

Hlobane Mountain and Khambula

Redvers Henry BULLER, Hlobane Mountain, 28 March 1879

Redvers Buller was born on 7 December 1839 in Crediton, Devon, the second of seven sons (there were also four daughters) to James Wentworth Buller MP and Charlotte Juliana, daughter of Lord Henry Howard. Redvers was educated at private schools, latterly at Eton. At 16 he arrived at Exeter railway station to be met by his mother, who was suffering from a haemorrhage. He attended to her in the waiting room but she died two days later.

Buller knew from an early age he wanted to join the army but it almost never happened after he cut his leg so badly the doctor wanted to amputate it.

Redvers Buller.

Buller announced he would rather die with two legs than live with one.

In May 1858 he joined the 60th Rifles as an ensign, and within two years was in China. He took part in the storming of the Taku Forts in August 1860 and also the occupation of Peking in October that year. Buller was promoted to lieutenant in December 1862 and joined the 4th Battalion at Quebec, Canada, learning much about soldiering from Colonel Robert Hawley. It was during this time that he met Lord Wolseley. He returned to England in 1869 and was promoted to captain. In May 1870 he joined Lord Wolseley's force for the Red River Expedition, becoming one of the Wolseley gang.

Buller was attending the Staff College in August 1873 when Lord Wolseley requested he join him as his chief intelligence officer for the Asante Expedition to West Africa. He took part in a number of engagements and was slightly wounded at Ordashu. Invalided home due to sickness, it was some time before he fully recovered.

Promoted to brevet major in March 1874, be became Deputy Assistant Adjutant General at Horse Guards in April of the same year. In January 1878, he was offered an appointment as Special Service Officer to Lord Chelmsford in South Africa. In April, Buller was placed in charge of the Frontier Light Horse, taking part in the Ninth Cape Frontier War, and was mentioned in despatches twice. He was about to take part in the campaign against Chief Sekhukhune but it was postponed due to a drought.

Buller and the Frontier Light Horse were attached to Sir Evelyn Wood's Flying Column for the invasion of Zululand and, during the advance on Hlobane, they did much vital work, protecting supply columns and raiding Zulu kraals. On 24 January, a messenger arrived with the news of the disaster at iSandlwana. With this news Wood decided to build a strong defensive position at Khambula, from which he could continue to raid and harass the Zulus.

In March, Lord Chelmsford took a force to relieve the British troops surrounded at Eshowe. As a diversion, Wood's Flying Column would attack Hlobane. In a two-pronged manoeuvre Colonel Russell attacked the western end of the mountain while Lieutenant Colonel Buller attacked the eastern end, with the intension of driving the enemy into the path of Russell. Dawn on 28 March 1879 saw Buller atop of Hlobane Mountain leading his men across the summit, when his attention was brought to a large body of Zulus, 20,000 strong, approaching from the south. Buller had no choice but to order a retreat; the Ntendeka Pass, which they were to use, was a dangerous descent for mounted troops at the best of times but during a panic was much harder. Buller rescued Captain Henry D'Arcy, who was retiring on foot, carrying him on his own horse. He then went back and saved Lieutenant Everitt, whose horse had been shot from under him. He also saved a trooper of the Frontier Light Horse when he too had lost his horse. Rallying his men, Buller rode time and time again at the Zulus, under heavy fire from shot and spear. The following day the Zulus attacked Wood's fortified position at Khambula. Buller took out two squadrons of the Light Horse to goad the warriors into the British position. Under devastating fire, the Zulus broke. Buller's Light Horse were used for the pursuit of the fleeing Zulus.

Buller was present at the Battle of Ulundi, stationed inside the British square, and with the 17th Lancers took part in the final pursuit of the enemy. He was mentioned in despatches a number of times during the campaign and his VC, gazetted on 17 June 1879, was presented to him by the Queen at Balmoral on 9 September that year.

In September 1879, Buller was appointed as ADC to the Queen, with the rank of colonel, and in March 1880 he was made a major on half pay in the 60th Rifles. Sir Evelyn Wood VC requested him to be his chief of staff in South Africa in February 1881. He arrived just after the British defeat at Majuba Hill, effectively ending the war. Buller was promoted to brigadier general and received the local rank of major general in March 1881. While back in England, he married Lady Greville Howard in August 1882, with whom he had a daughter the following year.

Lord Wolseley requested he join him as his chief intelligence officer for the Egyptian Campaign in 1882, and Buller was present at the Battle of Tel-el-Kebir. In July 1883 he became Assistant Adjutant General at the War Office. In 1884, he returned to Africa for the Saukim Expedition in the Sudan, commanding the 1st Infantry Brigade, leading it at El Tab on 29 February 1884. During the Battle of Tamai, on 13 March 1884, the British advanced in two squares, one of which broke under a fanatical assault by the Sudanese. As they were driven back they mistakenly fired on Buller's square. He showed great coolness and rallied the men, so much in fact that the broken square was able to rally itself too.

Buller took part in Wolseley's failed attempt to relieve Gordon in Khartoum in the Nile Expedition in 1884, being present at the Battle of Abu Klea on 17 January 1885. He was again mentioned in despatches. His next post was as Deputy Adjutant General at Horse Guards, being appointed in November 1885. Buller spent much of 1886–87 in Ireland, in a civilian capacity restoring order as Special Commissioner at County Kerry.

In October 1887 he returned to military duties as Quartermaster General, which resulted in the formation of the Army Service Corps. In October 1890 he took over Lord Wolseley's position as Adjutant General, a post he held until 1897, being promoted to lieutenant general in 1891. Buller was appointed honorary colonel of the 1st Volunteer Battalion, the Devonshire Regiment, in May 1894, and became colonel commandant of the King's Royal Rifle Corps (formerly the 60th Rifles) in July 1895.

Buller was offered the post of Commander-in-Chief, India in 1893 but declined it as he was hoping to be appointed C-in-C of the British Army. However, this post went to Lord Wolseley and Buller was bitterly disappointed. In October 1898 he succeeded the Duke of Connaught in command of the troops at Aldershot.

In 1889, war with the Boers seemed imminent and due to Buller's experience he was sent to South Africa as head of the Natal Field Force – some 70,000 men, the largest army ever to leave the shores of England. On his arrival he found that the Boers had made the first move by invading Natal. Ladysmith, Kimberly and Mafeking were all besieged. This changed his strategy and he sent one column under Lord Methuen to Kimberly and he would strike towards Ladysmith.

On 15 December 1899, Buller reached Colenso, where the Boers were well entrenched. Major General Fitzroy Hart on the left flank advanced not towards the Bridle Drift ford, but into the loop of the river having been wrongly told by his African guide that the only ford was there. Buller could see Hart's error and sent a galloper to warn him. His men were met by accurate fire from three sides and suffered heavy casualties. Meanwhile, Colonel Long, who had been ordered to get his guns into action 'well out of range of the enemy', moved them too close to the river and was well within the range of the Boers. Long's gunners now came under fire and Buller ordered them to be withdrawn. Seven Victoria Crosses were awarded to men trying to save the guns (see Chapter 8). Realising everything that could go wrong had gone wrong, Buller decided to withdraw. British casualties were 1,200, including Buller, who had received a shrapnel wound. Lord Methuen had also suffered a reverse at Magersfontein a few days before in what became known as Black Week.

Buller decided he was not strong enough to achieve his objective and sent a message to General White VC at Ladysmith, which was interpreted as suggesting he should surrender. This the government could not accept, so they sent Lord Roberts VC with reinforcements. Buller was now operating solely on the Natal sector while Roberts and Lord Kitchener took up the offensive. Making a wide sweep towards Ladysmith, Buller tried using a night attack at Spion Kop on 24 January 1900, but Sir Charles Warren's men were left exposed atop the hill, which resulted in the heaviest casualties of the war. This led to him being called 'Reverse Buller'. Suffering another reverse at Vaal Krantz in February,

Buller changed tactics. Now making better use of cover and artillery support (unlike others who continued to use frontal attacks in the open against magazine-fed rifles) he broke through on the Tugela Line in mid-February 1900 and entered Ladysmith on 28 May.

In August, Buller moved forward to confront the Boers under Louis Botha, who were now (as predicted by Buller) starting to fight a guerrilla war. He put them to flight at Bergendal and Belfast before entering the Boer stronghold at Lydenburg in September 1900. The Natal Field Force was broken up and Buller returned to England in November 1900, where he again took up command at Aldershot.

Buller is buried in the family plot at Holy Cross churchyard, Crediton, Devon.

In October 1900 he was given command of the 1st Army Corps. However, his appointment was questioned in the media as the corps should be led by someone who would lead it in war. The message he had sent to General White VC in Ladysmith was published in part in the press and Buller asked to be able to read out the whole message but was not allowed to. However, during a public luncheon, he made some inappropriate remarks in his defence which were considered to breach King's Regulations and he was removed from command.

Redvers Buller remained on the active list for five years, but spent the rest of his life in Devon. He died from carcinoma of the gall bladder and liver on 2 June 1908, and is buried in Holy Cross churchyard, family plot, Church Street, Crediton. His VC is held by the Royal Green Jackets Regiment Museum, Winchester, Hampshire.

Buller is related to the brothers Victor and Alexander Turner, both of whom were awarded the VC.

William Knox LEET, Hlobane Mountain, 28 March 1879

William Leet was born on 3 November 1833 in Dalkey, County Dublin, Ireland, one of five sons and two daughters to Edward Patrick Leet, rector of Dalkey, and Sarah Knox. All of their children bore the name Knox-Leet, but William is always listed under Leet, so he may have used Knox only as a middle name. All five boys served in the armed forces, William being commissioned into the 13th Light Infantry (later the Somerset Light Infantry) as an ensign in July 1855, and promoted to lieutenant in February 1856.

William Leet.

Leet was serving in the Cape Colony when the Indian Mutiny broke out and his regiment was posted to Calcutta. He saw active service with his battalion and as a staff officer under Lord Mark Kerr during the Central India and Trans-Gogra operations, including Gorakhpur and Oudh. He was present at Amorah on 17 and 25 April 1858, and was at Nugger on 29 April. For both of these actions he was mentioned in despatches. He was also present at Jugdespore, Toolespore, Tirhoot, Nepal Terai, and twice at Bootwall. Leet was adjutant of the 13th Light Infantry from August 1858 to June 1864.

There followed a long period in England and Ireland and he was promoted to captain in November 1864. In September 1871, he was appointed Musket Instructor at Hythe. The same year, he married Charlotte Sherlock and their first of two sons was born in 1873. Leet was Deputy Assistant Adjutant General and Quartermaster at Cork until 1877.

The 13th Light Infantry sailed for South Africa in April 1877, Leet joining them in October having been promoted to brevet major. The 13th were to take part in the advance to the stronghold of Chief Sekhukhune but, due to a drought, the expedition was called off. He joined Wood's column for the invasion of Zululand and when at the camp at Khambula took command of the 1st Battalion, Wood's Irregulars, a unit of disaffected Zulus. Before the column was involved in action, Leet had the misfortune to wrench his knee joint in a tug-of-war competition between officers of the 13th and 90th regiments.

On 28 March, Colonel Wood VC set out for Hlobane to attack the Zulu stronghold there. Wood suggested Leet remain at the camp due to his knee, but Leet insisted he would be okay as he would remain mounted. Lieutenant Colonel Russell would attack from the west while Lieutenant Colonel Redvers Buller's force would attack from the east. Wood and his small entourage made their way leisurely to the base of the mountain with the intention of following Buller's route to the summit. Once atop the mountain the Zulus could be seen outflanking their position, so they started to withdraw. During the retreat Lieutenant Alfred Smith's horse was killed from under him. Leet rode to him, and, under a shower of assegais and bullets, picked him up and carried him on his own horse to a place of safety.

The next day the Zulus attacked Wood's position at Khambula. Major Leet was in command of two companies of the 13th Light Infantry and a company of the 90th in the redoubt facing the Zulu attack. He was mentioned in despatches for his bravery at Hlobane and again for his conduct at Khambula. Leet was also present at the Battle of Ulundi. Lieutenant Smith said of him: 'Had it not been for Major Leet, nothing could have saved me, and I owe him the deepest gratitude, which I shall feel as long as I live.' Smith also presented Leet with a silver cup.

Leet's VC, gazetted on 17 June 1879, was presented to him by the Queen at Windsor Castle on 9 December 1879, the same day that William Allan and others received theirs. Leet was promoted to brevet lieutenant colonel in November 1879 and lieutenant colonel in July 1881. In May 1883, he took command of the 1st Battalion, Somerset Light Infantry. Leet was promoted to colonel in November 1883 and exchanged into the 2nd Battalion, which he commanded in the expedition

Leet's grave, St Mary the Virgin churchyard, Great Chart, Kent.

to Upper Burma in 1885–87. Unfortunately, many of his men died from disease.

William Leet retired in 1887 and settled in South London. He died on 29 June 1898 and is buried in St Mary the Virgin churchyard, Great Chart, Kent. His VC is held by the Somerset Light Infantry Museum, Taunton, Somerset.

Henry LYSONS, Hlobane Mountain, 28 March 1879

Henry Lysons was born on 13 July 1858 in Morden, Surrey, the second son of General Sir Daniel Lysons and Harriet Sophia (née Bridges). He was educated at Wellington College and in May 1878 joined the 90th Light Infantry as an ensign, and served as Sir Evelyn Wood's ADC throughout the Cape Frontier and Zulu War.

On the morning of 28 March 1879, Colonel Wood VC set out for Hlobane to attack the Zulu stronghold there. Lieutenant Colonel Russell would attack

Henry Lysons.

from the west while Lieutenant Colonel Redvers Buller's force would attack from the east. Wood and his small entourage (three staff officers and eight mounted men from the 90th) made their way leisurely to the base of the mountain with the intention of following Buller's route to the summit. As they proceeded up the pass following Buller they came under fire from Zulus hidden in caves above them. To Wood's horror, his trusted interpreter and political officer, Mr Llewellyn Lloyd, had been mortally wounded. Wood had him taken to a nearby kraal, where most of the party had taken cover. Advancing again, Wood's horse was shot from under him, pinning him down. It took him a few minutes to free himself and he ordered the Border Horse to flush out the Zulus. There was a delay in them carrying out the order, so Captain Campbell, Lieutenant Lysons and Private Fowler of the escort charged in, but Campbell was killed by a point-blank shot.

Colonel Wood seems to have had something of a mental breakdown at this point as, with an uncontrolled battle raging on the plateau above him and a large Zulu force approaching him, he went into meltdown and ordered his two friends to be buried, and for his bugler Walkinshaw to fetch his bible from his dead horse. With no digging tools, Wood ordered his Zulu irregulars to use their assegais to dig the graves. When the two bodies were lowered in, the grave was too short and some further digging was needed; when it was filled in, Wood read a short service.

Once atop the mountain the Zulus could be seen outflanking their position, so they started to withdraw. The next day, the Zulus attacked Wood's position at Khambula and Wood was able to inflict a major defeat upon them. Lysons took part in this action and distinguished himself. Lysons was with the men sent to recover the body of the Prince Imperial on 1 June. He also took part in the final battle of the war at Ulundi on 4 July 1879.

He was adjutant of the 90th Light Infantry from 1880 to 1882 and was in India when his VC was gazetted on 7 April 1882. It was presented to him by Colonel Craig at Cawnpore, on 18 August 1882. Lysons was employed with the Egyptian Army under Lord Wolseley from February 1884 to October 1885 and took part in the failed Nile Expedition to relieve General Gordon at Khartoum.

Back in England, Lysons served as ADC to Brigadier General Dunne, commanding officer of the 2nd Infantry Brigade at Aldershot, from February 1886 to March 1887, and was promoted to captain in June 1886. He was appointed Garrison Adjutant at Dublin, June 1887 to January 1889, and was Adjutant of the Volunteers from September 1888 to November 1893. He passed his final exam at the Staff College at Sandhurst in 1890 and returned to Aldershot as ADC to the General Officer Commanding, June 1891 to October 1893.

In November 1895 Lysons was appointed Deputy Assistant Adjutant General under Lord Wolseley. Lysons married Vanda Treffry, who was sixteen years his junior. In

Lysons' grave, St Peter's churchyard, Rodmarton, Gloucestershire.

December 1900 he was promoted to lieutenant colonel and commanded the 1st Battalion, the Bedfordshire Regiment. His last appointment was as Assistant Quartermaster General, Eastern Command HQ, India, with the rank of colonel.

Henry Lysons retired from the army on half pay in January 1906 and returned to England. He died on 24 July 1907 and is buried in St Peter's churchyard, Rodmarton, near Cirencester, Gloucestershire. His VC is held by the Cameronians Museum, Hamilton, Lanarkshire.

Edmund John FOWLER, Hlobane Mountain, 28 March 1879

Edmund Fowler was born in 1861 at Waterford, Ireland, the son of John and Bridget Fowler. He worked as a trade servant prior to enlisting into the 90th Light Infantry in March 1877. The 90th embarked for South Africa and Fowler went with them, taking part in the Ninth Cape Frontier War.

After the first invasion of Zululand and the disaster at iSandlwana, Colonel Wood VC was given the job of harassing the Zulus while Lord Chelmsford prepared for the second invasion. On the morning of 28 March 1879, Colonel Wood VC set out for Hlobane to attack the Zulu stronghold there. Lieutenant Colonel Russell would attack from the west while Lieutenant Colonel Redvers Buller's force would attack from the east. Wood and his small entourage (three staff officers and eight mounted men from the 90th) made their way leisurely to the base of the mountain with the intention of following Buller's route to the summit. As they proceeded up the pass following Buller they came under fire from Zulus hidden in caves above them. To Wood's horror, his trusted interpreter and political officer, Mr Llewellyn Lloyd, had been mortally wounded. Wood had him taken to a nearby kraal, where most of the party had taken cover. Advancing again, Wood's horse was shot from under him, pinning him down. It took him a few

Edmund Fowler.

minutes to free himself and he ordered the Border Horse to flush out the Zulus. As there was a delay in them carrying out the order, Captain Campbell, together with another staff officer, Lieutenant Lysons and Private Fowler of the escort, charged in, but Campbell was killed by a point-blank shot.

The next day at the Battle of Khambula, Fowler was stationed close to Sir Evelyn Wood VC. Fowler had been trying to hit a Zulu chief but could not seem to get the range, so he asked the colonel for help. Wood took the rifle, adjusted the sights and killed the Zulu. He then shot two more Zulus with his rifle before handing it back. He took part in the final battle of the war at Ulundi on 4 July 1879.

Fowler was discharged from the army in January 1880 and he married Mary McGuire; they went on to have five children. His VC, gazetted on 7 April 1882, was presented to him by the Queen at Windsor Castle on 13 April 1882. Later that year he re-enlisted into the 2nd Battalion, the Royal Irish Regiment. He served in the Sudan Campaign of 1884–85 with the Egyptian Army and in the failed attempt to relieve General Gordon at Khartoum.

By 1887, Fowler was a colour sergeant but he was court-martialled and the Secretary of State for War asked to have his name removed from the Victoria Cross register after he was convicted of embezzlement. The Queen refused to do so as the sole punishment of the court was for him to be reduced to the ranks and it appeared to her that his offence was not too serious.

Fowler finally left the army in 1900. He sold his VC for £42 in 1906 but retained a duplicate to wear. He ran a fruiterer's shop and later was a

Fowler's grave, Colchester Cemetery, Essex.

pub landlord. In 1920 he attended the VC garden party at Buckingham Palace and in the same year he was present at the memorial service held at the cenotaph in Whitehall.

Edmund Fowler died on 26 March 1926 and is buried in Colchester Cemetery, Section Q, Grave 12–42, Mersea Road, Colchester, Essex. His VC is held by the Cameronians Museum, Hamilton, Lanarkshire.

Edward Stevenson BROWNE, Khambula, 29 March 1879

Edward Browne was born on 23 December 1852 in Cambridge, the son of Salwey Browne, a student at Cambridge University and an officer in the 68th Regiment, and his wife Elizabeth Browne (née Stevenson). He was educated at the Royal Military Academy, Sandhurst, from August 1869 to December 1870. He was commissioned an ensign in the 24th Regiment of Foot on 23 September 1871, and promoted to lieutenant in the 1st Battalion in October of the same year.

Edward Browne.

Browne sailed with his battalion to Malta in January 1872, and then on to Gibraltar two months later. In 1874 he was posted to South Africa and took part in the Griqualand West Expedition of 1875. He was one of a detachment of the 24th, who formed the 1st Squadron of Imperial Mounted Infantry under Lieutenant Frederick Carrington and was sent to Natal In April 1877. Browne took part in the Ninth Cape Frontier War and later joined Colonel Rowlands VC for an expedition against Chief Sekhukhune and the Pedi tribe. However, due to a serious drought, the expedition was called off.

The Mounted Infantry joined No. 3 Column for the invasion of Zululand and formed the escort for Lord Chelmsford when he moved north to meet with Colonel Wood VC. On the following day, Lieutenant Browne led the Mounted Infantry in a skirmish against Chief Sihayo and arrived at iSandlwana on 20 January 1879. On the morning of the

Hlobane Mountain and Khambula 53

21st, Browne carried out a reconnaissance beyond Isiphezi Hill. Seeing some Zulus in the distance and another party of Zulus, he attempted to cut them off. Shots were exchanged and Browne returned to camp and reported what he had seen, not realising those warriors were a scouting party for the main Zulu army. On the 24th, Browne was part of Lord Chelmsford's escort when he left iSandlwana to look for the Zulu army, returning that night after the disastrous battle and having to spend the night among the dead. He was also present when Lord Chelmsford arrived at Rorke's Drift on the morning of 23 January.

Having now joined Sir Evelyn Wood's Flying Column he took part in the Battle of Hlobane on 28 March, and on the following day, at the Battle of Khambula, he saved the life of Colonel Russell, who had become unseated from his horse (his citation incorrectly states his VC action was on 28 March at Hlobane).

His VC, gazetted on 17 June 1897, was presented to him by Lord Wolseley at Utrecht on 22 August 1979, in the same investiture as Major Bromhead's. Browne took part in Lord Wolseley's campaign against Sekhukhune in October 1879. On his return to England he married Amelia Wright in November 1879, and they had two sons and two daughters.

Browne was promoted to captain in May 1880, and became adjutant of the 3rd Battalion, Mounted Rifle Volunteers, from September 1881 to September 1886, during which time he was promoted to major. Browne's next appointment was as Deputy Assistant Adjutant General of Musketry in Bengal, India, from November 1891 to July 1892. He was promoted to lieutenant colonel in April 1893 and appointed colonel, Officer Commanding the 24th Regimental District, Brecon, in April 1897. In March 1900 he was appointed Officer Commanding the 5th Army Corps in York. On 7 September 1902 he was promoted to temporary brigadier general and became honorary colonel of the West Yorkshire Regiment in December 1902. He took over command of the 6th and 11th Infantry Brigades, 2nd Army Corps, Southern Command, in June 1904.

Edward Browne retired from the army in November 1906 and settled in Southsea, near Portsmouth. He died from heart disease on 16 July 1907 and is buried in an unmarked grave, Clarens Cemetery, Protestant Section (grave reused in 1991 and the headstone was broken up), Chemin de Muraz, Montreux, Switzerland. His VC is held by the Regimental Museum of the Royal Welsh, Brecon, Powys.

Chapter 5

Ulundi

William Leslie de la Poer 'Ulundi' BERESFORD, Ulundi, 3 July 1879

William Beresford was born on 20 July 1847 in Mullaghbrack, County Armagh, Ireland. He was the third son of five to John de la Poer Beresford, rector of Mullaghbrack, who became 4th Marques of Waterford in 1859, and Christiana, daughter of Colonel Charles Leslie MP. He was educated at Eaton in 1858, being described as having a 'turbulent disposition'.

In 1863 he went to Bonn to study French and German at the home of Doctor Perry. While on a hiking trip to the Austrian Tyrol in 1866 with his tutor and a group of boys, they became lost and spent the night in a hut. Doctor Perry went out to find the nearest village, but got into difficulty. Realising something was wrong, Beresford went in search of him, making a number of attempts to find him and eventually rescuing him from a perilous position.

William Beresford.

Beresford entered the 9th Queen's Royal Lancers as a cornet and was promoted to lieutenant in June 1870. He was posted to India in 1874, becoming ADC on the staff of Viceroy Northbrook the following year. He was promoted to captain in December 1876 and given leave to take part in the Jowaki Expedition of 1877–78 under General Keyes. Granted leave again, he was able to rejoin his regiment to take part in the storming of the Ali Musjid Citadel in the later part of the Afghan War, being mentioned in despatches.

Having returned to his duties as ADC in Calcutta, he heard the news about the defeat at iSandlwana. Beresford was granted six months' leave to go to South Africa, arriving in Durban in April 1879. He was appointed ADC to Colonel Buller, and joined his Flying Column for the second invasion of Zululand.

On 3 July 1879, Beresford, Captain D'Arcy, Sergeant Edmund O'Toole and others were carrying out a reconnaissance when attacked by a large body of Zulus. During the retirement Beresford went to the assistance of Sergeant Fitzmaurice, whose horse had fallen and rolled on top of him, only a few yards from the pursuing Zulus. Fitzmaurice urged him to ride on and save himself. Beresford told him, 'If you don't get up, I'll punch your head in!' As he helped him into his saddle they were joined by Sergeant O'Toole, who rode alongside, shooting Zulu after Zulu as well as holding the wounded man up in his saddle until they all reached safety.

The following day saw the climactic end to the Zulu War at the Battle of Ulundi. Beresford was inside the British square and after the battle was over, the mounted troops approached the king's kraal. Spurred on by Beresford's call of 'Who will be the first into Ulundi?' a number of officers raced for the gate, but Beresford jumped his horse over the Kraal fence and was known as 'Ulundi Beresford' for the rest of his life.

Beresford's VC, gazetted on 23 August 1879, was presented to him by the Queen at Osborne House. He told her that he could not in honour receive the award unless it was shared with D'Arcy and O'Toole. She was so impressed with his chivalry that she made enquires and both men were subsequently awarded it.

On his return to India in June 1881, Beresford took up his role as ADC. In January 1886, now a major, he accompanied Lord Dufferin during the Third Burma War and was mentioned in despatches and promoted to brevet lieutenant colonel. He returned to India and served out the remainder of his career there, retiring on half pay in 1894.

Beresford was a keen horse rider all of his life and had numerous racing successes with a number of his horses. He married Lilian Warren, daughter of Cicero Price, a US Navy commodore, in April 1895, and they had one son, to whom William was devoted. They lived at Deepdene, Dorking, where they received many visitors, including Edward, Prince of Wales, and Winston Churchill.

In December 1896 William Beresford had a serious riding accident, falling from his horse and breaking his pelvis. Already weak from bouts of dysentery, he never fully recovered. He became ill with peritonitis and suffered a heart attack, and died on 28 December 1900. He is buried in Clonagem churchyard, Curraghmore, Co. Waterford. His VC is not publicly held.

Henry Cecil Dudgeon D'ARCY, Ulundi, 3 July 1879

Henry D'Arcy.

Henry D'Arcy was born on 11 August 1850 in Wanganui, New Zealand, the seventh of nine children to Major Oliver Barker D'Arcy and Angelica Martha. His father emigrated to South Africa after taking part in the Maori Wars of the 1860s, settling in King William's Town in the Cape.

Not much is known of Henry's early life but he was employed as a clerk in the Civil Service prior to enlisting into the Albany Mounted Volunteers at the outbreak of the Cape Frontier War in 1877. When the fighting was over the unit was disbanded and D'Arcy joined the Frontier Light Horse. He was promoted to lieutenant in December 1877 and, during a confrontation with Chief Sandile's Gaikas when a sniper had pinned down the men, D'Arcy climbed onto a barrel to attract his fire while one of his men shot the sniper. He was present at the funeral of Chief Sandile in June 1878.

In 1879, the Frontier Light Horse were assigned to No. 4 Column for the invasion of Zululand. D'Arcy took part in a number of skirmishes and then, on 27 March, the Light Horse set out for Hlobane to attack the Zulu stronghold there. Once atop the mountain the Zulus could be seen outflanking their position, so they started to withdraw. D'Arcy was unseated from his horse and was almost ridden down by another. Trooper Francis caught a horse for D'Arcy and, as they were fleeing the Zulus, he heard the cries of another trooper with a serious leg wound. D'Arcy dismounted and helped the man onto his own horse and continued on foot. As the Zulus were closing in Colonel Buller appeared and told him to mount behind him. D'Arcy said to leave him, Buller told him not to be a fool, and the two men rode back together. Both men were recommended for the Victoria Cross by Sir Evelyn Wood VC, but only Buller's was approved. The following day at the Battle of Khambula the Zulus were defeated and the Light Horse pursued the fleeing warriors.

On 3 July 1879, D'Arcy, Beresford, O'Toole and others were carrying out a reconnaissance when attacked by a large body of Zulus. During the retirement D'Arcy saw Trooper Raubenheim fall from his horse. He stopped and picked him up, but the horse kicked them both off, injuring D'Arcy's back. Raubenheim was stunned and D'Arcy made several vain attempts to lift him back into the saddle as the Zulus closed in. Eventually he was forced to ride on alone. Due to his back injury he was unable to take part in the Battle of Ulundi.

D'Arcy's VC, gazetted on 9 October 1879 (after the intervention of Beresford), was presented to him by Lord Wolseley at Pretoria on 10 December 1879. After the Frontier Light Horse were disbanded, D'Arcy was promoted to captain in the Cape Mounted Rifles (his father's old regiment). He served with distinction in the Basuto Rebellion in 1880–81 but, due to a disagreement, he resigned in April 1881, saying it was 'of a private nature'.

Henry D'Arcy went missing on 5 August 1881 while in a state of delirium, and his remains were found three months later in the Amatola Forest. He is buried in King William's Town Cemetery, Section D, Grave 32–33, family plot, Cape Province, South Africa. However, a note discovered in the Killie Campbell Africana Library in 1980 suggested that he may have changed clothes with a dead man. He was said to have been recognised from a photograph fifty-six years later in Natal. When confronted, he begged the man not to make his identity known, wishing 'to remain dead to the world'. His VC is not publicly held.

Edmund Joseph O'TOOLE, Ulundi, 3 July 1879

Possibly the most obscure of all VC recipients, Edmund O'Toole was born in Ireland, perhaps in 1848, as it is known he was baptised in Dublin in that year. Almost nothing is known of his early life before he enlisted into the Frontier Light Horse with Henry D'Arcy in 1877. He fought in the Cape Frontier War of 1877–78, taking part in a number of skirmishes. He was also present at the funeral of Chief Sandile in June 1878.

In 1879 the Frontier Light Horse were assigned to No. 4 Column for the invasion of Zululand. Now a sergeant, O'Toole took part in a number of skirmishes, and then on 27 March he was involved in the assault on Hlobane to attack the Zulu stronghold there. The following day he took part in the Battle of Khambula; the Light Horse goaded the Zulus into attacking the British position. As they fell back Trooper Elliot was unhorsed and O'Toole returned to help him remount. After the Zulus were defeated he took part in the pursuit of the routing Zulus.

Edmund O'Toole.

On 3 July 1879, O'Toole, Beresford, D'Arcy, and others were carrying out a reconnaissance when attacked by a large body of Zulus. During the retirement D'Arcy rode alongside Captain Beresford, keeping the pursuing Zulus back with steady fire and holding the wounded Sergeant Fitzmaurice in the saddle until they all reached safety. They were joined by Sergeant O'Toole, who rode alongside, shooting Zulu after Zulu, as well as holding the wounded man up in his saddle.

O'Toole's VC, gazetted on 9 October 1879 (after the intervention of Beresford), was presented to him by Lord Wolseley at Pretoria on 10 December 1879. After the Frontier Light Horse were disbanded he joined the Herschel Native Contingent as a captain in October 1880 and took part in a rebellion in Rhodesia. He also saw service with the Protectorate Police.

Edmund O'Toole reportedly died in Salisbury (now Harare), Zimbabwe, in 1891, but has no known grave. However, his name appears in 'The Black and White Budget', dated August 1900, being on a list of VC recipients living in South Africa, referring to him as 'a resident of the Cape'. His VC is not publicly held.

Part 2

The First Boer War

After the end of the Zulu War in 1879, Britain failed to deliver the desired federal dominion of British colonies and Boer republics. There was growing tension between the British and the Boers. Britain was not prepared to give back territory of the Transvaal that had been annexed, and the Boer resentment was escalated by the revenue-collecting activities of the Administrator of the Transvaal. This, along with allegations of undisciplined behaviour by British troops, drove the Boers to boiling point, and on 16 December 1880 they declared a republic. Six Victoria Crosses were awarded for this campaign.

Chapter 6

Elandsfontein, Laing's Nek, Wasselstroom and Mujaba Mountain

James MURRAY, Elandsfontein, 16 January 1881

James Murray was born in February 1859 in St Michael's Parish, Cork, Ireland. He enlisted in the 2nd Battalion, Connaught Rangers and was posted to South Africa, arriving just in time for the outbreak of the war.

At dawn on 16 January 1881, a mounted column under the command of Colonel Gildea left Pretoria and came across the Boers at Elandsfontein. British artillery bombarded the Boer position for twenty minutes and then the 94th advanced. Suffering heavy casualties they were ordered to retire by Colonel Bellairs, and it was noticed that some men were missing,

James Murray.

believed to be lying wounded near the enemy position. Lance Corporal Murray and Trooper Danaher advanced into the open under heavy fire to the assistance of two wounded men, Byrne and Davies. Murray's horse was shot almost immediately and they advanced 500 yards on foot. On reaching Byrne, Murray was wounded by a bullet that entered his right side and exited near his spine. Murray ordered Danaher to take his carbine and make good his escape. Shortly after, Byrne died, and Murray and Davies were taken prisoner but released the next day, along with Byrne's body. Davies died a few days later.

Murray and Danaher were both awarded the VC, gazetted on 14 March 1882, Murray being presented with his on 15 May by the Queen at

Windsor Castle. Little is known about the rest of his life, other than he returned to Ireland.

James Murray died on 19 July 1942 and is buried in Glasnevin Cemetery, Finglas Road, Dublin. His VC is held by the National Army Museum, London.

John DANAHER (DANAGHER on his citation), Elandsfontein, 16 January 1881

John Danaher was born on 25 June 1860 in Limerick, Ireland. He was educated at the Christian Brothers, Limerick. He joined the Connaught Rangers in April 1880, and shortly after was on his way to South Africa for service in the Boer War.

At dawn on 16 January 1881, a mounted column under the command of Colonel Gildea left Pretoria and came across the Boers at Elandsfontein. British artillery bombarded the Boer position for twenty minutes and then the 94th advanced. Suffering heavy casualties they were ordered to retire by Colonel Bellairs, and it was noticed that some men were missing, believed to be lying wounded near the enemy position. Troopers Murray and Danaher advanced into the open under heavy fire to the assistance of two wounded men, Byrne and Davies. Murray's horse was shot almost immediately and they advanced 500 yards on foot. On reaching Byrne, Murray was wounded by a bullet that entered his right side and exited near his spine. Murray ordered Danaher to take his carbine and make good his escape. Shortly after, Byrne died, and Murray and Davies were taken

John Danaher.

Danaher's (Danagher) grave, Milton Cemetery, Portsmouth, Hampshire.

prisoner but released the next day, along with Byrne's body. Davies died a few days later.

Danaher and Murray were both awarded the VC, gazetted on 14 March 1882; Danaher was presented with his on 23 August by Viceroy Curragh in Ireland. He was discharged from the army with a pension, married and had six sons, all of whom served in the First World War, one being killed at Gallipoli in 1915. Another was a POW and a third was wounded.

In later life John Danaher lived on the south coast of England and was landlord of the Dog & Duck public house in Portsmouth. He died on 9 January 1919 and is buried in Milton Cemetery, Plot M, Row 1, Grave 6, Milton Road, Portsmouth, Hampshire. His VC is held by the National Army Museum, London.

Alan Richard HILL (later HILL-WALKER), Laing's Nek, 28 January 1881

Alan Hill was born on 12 July 1859 in Northallerton, Yorkshire, the oldest son of Captain Thomas Hill, Chief Constable of the North Riding. He was educated at Richmond Grammar School and joined the North York Rifles in 1877, transferring to the 59th (Rutlandshire) Regiment of Foot (later the Northamptonshire Regiment) in 1879. With this regiment he served throughout the Zulu War, taking part in the final battle at Ulundi on 4 July 1879.

Alan Hill.

On the morning of 28 January 1881 at Laing's Nek, British artillery bombarded the Boer position on Table Hill and ten minutes later, Colonel Deane led the 58th with Lieutenant Baillie carrying the regimental colour (this was the last time British troops carried their standards into battle, although some historians claim it was at Tel-el-Kebir in 1882 or in Burma in 1942). Baillie was wounded and Hill went to his assistance. Baillie called out, 'Never mind me, save the Colours,' and Hill passed the colours to another man and, as he was unable to lift Baillie onto a horse, he carried him in his arms until he died. Hill then returned and recovered another wounded man, all the time under a heavy fire.

Hill was also in action at Ingogo and Majuba, being severely wounded at the latter. He was mentioned in despatches and awarded the VC, gazetted on 14 March 1882. Hill was presented with his VC on 13 May 1882 by the Queen at Windsor Castle. In 1883 and 1885, he served in Natal and Cape Town, becoming adjutant of the 3rd and 4th battalions of the Northampton Militia from 1887 to 1892. For the next three years, Hill was Station Staff Officer at Bangalore, India, and performed a similar role in Mandalay in 1897. He also took part in the Tirah Expedition 1897–98, marching down the Bara Valley.

In 1902, Hill married Muriel Lillian Walker and changed his name to Hill-Walker. They had two sons, one of whom was killed in action in 1940. During his retirement, Hill-Walker enjoyed hunting and shooting. Alan Hill died on 21 April 1944 and is buried in St Michael and All Angels churchyard, Maunby, near Thirsk, Yorkshire. His VC is in the Ashcroft Gallery, Imperial War Museum, London.

John DOOGAN, Laing's Nek, 28 January 1881

John Doogan was born in March 1853 in Aughrim, County Galway, Ireland. Very little is known about his early life but he enlisted into the 1st Dragoon Guards (The King's) circa 1873, and had been posted to South Africa by 1880.

On the morning of 28 January 1881 at Laing's Nek, Doogan took part in a charge of mounted men. During the charge Major Brownlow's horse had been shot from under him and he had fallen among the Boers. Doogan, although wounded, rode to Major Brownlow, dismounted and persuaded the major to take his horse. Doogan was wounded again at this time but both men managed to escape.

John Doogan.

For this action Doogan was awarded the VC, gazetted on 14 March 1882, and was presented with it in May by the Superintendant of Pensions at Cork. Doogan married twice and had two sons, both of whom were killed in action during the First World War. In 1891 he was working for the Post Office as a driver and by 1901 he was living in England, working as a butler in Berkshire. By 1911 he was he was living in Shropshire and from 1926 to 1937 he worked as a farmer.

John Doogan died on 24 January 1940 and is buried in Shorncliffe Military Cemetery (aka Garrison Cemetery), Plot V, Grave 1054, Hospital Hill, on the B2063, in Folkestone, Kent. His medals passed to his family, who, after the end of the Second World War, presented them to the colonel of the Dragoon's regiment in Cardiff Castle, where they were put on display in the sergeants' mess. In 1956 the medals were loaned to the organisers of the VC Centenary Exhibition. Shortly after this the regiment was posted overseas and the medals were forgotten and assumed lost. Then, in 1997, the colonel of the regiment received a letter from a London bank requesting he pick up two parcels from the bank's vault addressed to the regiment. When the parcels were opened, Doogan's medals were found to be inside, and after 41 years, they are now in the Queen's Dragoon Guards Museum, Cardiff.

Doogan's grave, Shorncliffe Military Cemetery, Folkestone, Kent.

James OSBORNE, Wasselstroom, 22 February 1881

James Osborne was born on 13 April 1857 in Wigginton, near Tring, Hertfordshire. Nothing is known about his early life until he enlisted into the 2nd Battalion, 58th Northamptonshire Regiment, circa 1878.

In 1881 Osborne was part of the garrison at Wasselstroom (aka Wakkerstroom) when, during a skirmish on 22 February, he galloped out in the direction of a large force of Boers, some forty strong. He picked up Private Mayes, who was lying wounded, and brought him back to camp under heavy fire. For this action he was awarded the VC, gazetted on 14 March. There is no record of an investiture so the medal was probably posted to him!

On his return to Wigginton after the war Osborne took up a job as a labourer on the Rothschild Estate, working there for twenty-six years. In 1913 he suffered a stroke, which left him partly paralysed. Osborne died on 2 February 1928 and is buried in St Bartholomew's churchyard, Hemp Lane, Wigginton.

James Osborne.

Upon his death, James Osborne's VC passed to his regiment. During the Second World War the regiment placed its silver and other precious items, including Osborne's VC, into the Ulster Bank vault for safe keeping, but it was destroyed in an air raid in April 1941. In 1964, Osborne's daughter asked about the medal's whereabouts and was told of its destruction. No official replacement was ever requested by her. In 2008, his granddaughter requested a replacement but was told under the rules governing this that only his direct next of kin could apply for an official replacement.

Osborne's grave, St Bartholomew's churchyard, Wigginton, Hertfordshire.

Joseph John FARMER, Majuba Mountain, 27 February 1881

Joseph John Farmer was born on 5 May 1855 in Clerkenwell, London. He left school at 10 years of age and went to sea. In 1878 he contracted smallpox and was hospitalised in Hampstead Heath, later being employed as a hospital porter.

Farmer served in the Anglo-Zulu War, treating some of the Zulu wounded from the Battle of Ulundi, and then served at Newcastle before going to the Transvaal with a field hospital. He almost drowned when crossing the flooded Ingogo River.

Farmer accompanied General Colley's force during a night march up Majuba Mountain overlooking the Boer camp near the Transvaal border. At dawn on 27 February 1881, the Boers saw that the British had occupied the crest of the hill and started a three-pronged attack. Their superior firepower forced the British to retire, and as the Boers fought their way to the top of the hill, Colley was shot, apparently by Piet Uys's 12-year-old son.

Joseph Farmer.

Boer rounds started to fall among the British wounded and Surgeon Landon, who was paralysed by a bullet, ordered Farmer to try to stop the Boers from firing on the hospital area. Farmer, who was slightly wounded, stood up and started waving a white bandage to indicate that it was a hospital area. He was shot through the hand and reportedly said, 'I have another,' and waved the bandage with his other hand until he was shot through the elbow, but his actions stopped the Boers firing on the wounded.

For this action Farmer was awarded the VC, gazetted on 17 May 1881. He was presented with it on 9 August 1881 by the Queen at Osborne House. Due to his wounds Farmer left the Army Hospital Corps and joined the Corps of Commissionaires. He also took up work as a house painter. He married and had a son.

Joseph Farmer died on 30 June 1930 and is buried in Brompton Cemetery, Compartment H, 157′ × 4′3″, Old Brompton Road, London. His very impressive headstone is a boulder from Majuba Mountain. His VC is held by the Museum of Military Medicine, Keogh Barracks, Aldershot, Surrey.

Farmer's grave, Brompton Cemetery, London.

Part 3

The Second Boer War

Having subjugated the southern African tribes to create the colonies of Natal and Cape Colony, Britain now wanted to bring together her colonies and Boer republics, the Orange Free State and the Transvaal into one British-dominated South African Federation.

The Dutch-speaking Boers, whose population was now in the majority, had already suffered incursions from outsiders, mostly British. After gold was discovered in the Transvaal in 1886, the Boers were unwilling to lose their independence. Seventy-eight Victoria Crosses were awarded for this campaign.

Chapter 7

Siege of Mafeking and Ladysmith

Charles 'Fitz' FITZCLARENCE, Mafeking, 14 & 27 October, 26 December 1899

Charles Fitzclarence was born on 8 May 1865 in Bishopscourt, Country Kildare, Ireland, the son of Captain George Fitzclarence of the Royal Navy. His mother was Maria Henrietta Scott, the eldest daughter of the 4th Earl of Clonmel. His father was one of four brothers who served in either the army or the navy, one of them being killed in the assault on the Redan during the Crimea War. Charles's twin brother Edward was killed at Abu Hamed, Egypt, in 1887. His paternal grandfather was George Augustus Frederick Fitzclarence, 1st Earl of Munster, an illegitimate son of William, Duke of Clarence (later William IV of England).

Charles Fitzclarence.

He was educated at Eton and Wellington colleges. He was gazetted a lieutenant from the Militia into the Royal Fusiliers in November 1886. During Kitchener's Khartoum Campaign, he was adjutant of the Mounted Infantry Regiment in Egypt. When the troops moved up the Nile in support, the Mounted Infantry were left behind, much to his disappointment. Promoted to captain in April 1898, he married Violet, youngest daughter of Lord Alfred Spencer Churchill MP and granddaughter of George Spencer-Churchill (6th Duke of Marlborough). They had two children, Edward Charles and Joan Harriet.

Fitzclarence was sent to South Africa in 1899 on special service and was present at the siege of Mafeking, where his gallantry and daring earned him the name 'The Demon' from Robert Baden-Powell. He was serving in the Royal Fusiliers, attached to the Bechuanaland Protectorate Regiment, when, on 14 October, he went to the assistance of an armoured train with a partially trained squadron. The enemy were in greatly superior numbers and he was for a time surrounded. Fitzclarence so inspired his men that, not only was the train relieved, but they killed fifty Boers and wounded many more. His own casualties were two killed and fifteen wounded.

On 27 October Fitzclarence led a night attack with the bayonet against the Boer trenches with sixty men. He was the first man to reach the enemy and killed four of them personally. The Boers retreated and in their panic fired on their own men; 150 Boers were killed or wounded. Fitzclarence's own casualties were six killed and nine wounded, with Fitz himself being slightly wounded. Major General Baden-Powell stated that, had this officer not shown an extraordinary spirit and fearlessness, both of the attacks would have failed, and we would have suffered heavy loss of men and prestige.

On 26 December Fitzclarence led an attack on a Boer stronghold known as 'Game Tree Fort'. The enemy fired constantly through loopholes. According to one report, 'Fitzclarence alone got inside and stabbed two or three. They shot him once, but he proceeded to bayonet another when they shot him a second time and he dropped down … though not dead.' He had in fact been severely wounded in both legs.

For these actions during the siege of Mafeking Fitzclarence was recommended for the Victoria Cross (gazetted on 6 July 1900). He was presented with his VC on 25 October 1900 by Lord Roberts VC at Pretoria. For his service in South Africa, Fritz was mentioned in despatches, given the brevet rank of major, and received the Queen's South Africa Medal with three clasps. Shortly after, he transferred into the newly formed Irish Guards.

From April 1903 to March 1905, Fitzclarence was Brigade Major of the 5th Brigade at Aldershot. In July 1909, he was given command of the 1st Battalion, Irish Guards. In 1913 he was appointed to the command of the regiment and regimental district, a post he held until the outbreak of the First World War. He then took over command of the 29th Brigade, 10th Division. On 27 September 1914, he took command of the 1st Guards Brigade with the British Expeditionary Force (BEF) in France.

On 14 October his brigade was holding trenches opposite the German line at the Aisne River; Fitzclarence ordered the Coldstream Guards to carry out a raid at night against a position known as 'Fish Hook Trench'. This was the first trench raid of the war and was a striking success. Later that month he played a significant part in the First Battle of Ypres, north of Gheluvelt, where his brigade suffered heavy casualties. The odds were against the British, with 24,000 Germans attacking 5,000 British along the Menin Road. In two days of fighting the Scots Guards alone lost ten officers and 370 men killed and wounded, but the British stood firm and unbroken while the Germans suffered enormous losses. Fitzclarence gave the order to counter-attack on the 31st, rallying the men and directing the successful onslaught.

On the morning of 11 November, thirteen battalions of Prussian Guards attacked along the Menin Road, but only in three places did they break through. The next morning Fitzclarence counter-attacked, with he himself leading the way. He was killed in action and has no known grave; Brigadier General Charles Fitzclarence is the highest-ranking officer to be named on the Menin Gate, Panel 3. His VC is in the Ashcroft Gallery, Imperial War Museum, London.

Robert JOHNSTON, Elandslaagte, 21 October 1899

Robert Johnston was born on 13 August 1872 in Laputa, County Donegal, Ireland, the son of Robert Johnston QC. Robert Jnr was educated at King William's College on the Isle of Man. He served in the 5th Battalion, Royal Inniskilling Fusiliers from 1890–94. During his time he was also a rugby union player for Ireland, making his international debut on 4 February 1893 in a 4–0 defeat against England, and a 2–0 defeat against Wales on 11 March. In 1896, Johnston was a member of the British Lions squad for their tour of South Africa, playing in three of the four tests against South Africa.

Robert Johnston.

After the tour ended he and Thomas Crean (who would also go on to be awarded the VC, see Chapter 11) decided to stay on and played rugby for the Transvaal, and Johnston captained the team in the Currie Cup. At the start of the Boer War in 1899 he and Thomas Crean enlisted into the Imperial Light Horse.

In October 1899 the Boers captured Elandslaagte Station, thus cutting off Ladysmith. Lieutenant General Sir George White sent his cavalry commander, Major General John French, to recapture the station. Arriving shortly after dawn on the 21st, they found the Boers in some strength with two field guns. French called up re-enforcements, which quickly arrived by train. British artillery bombarded the Boer position before assaulting it, and the Imperial Light Horse charged on foot. At a most critical moment, the advance was met with such a terrific fire that the men wavered for an instant. Johnston, with Captain Mullins, rushed forward through a hail of bullets and rallied the men, thus enabling the flanking movement to succeed. Johnston was wounded and was nursed back to health by Crean. Both Johnston and Mullins were mentioned in despatches and their VCs were gazetted on 12 February 1901. Johnston was wounded again during the siege of Ladysmith.

Johnston arrived in England in 1901 and was presented with his VC, together with Mullins, by Edward VII on 25 July 1901. He was also awarded the Queen's South Africa Medal with clasps for Elandslaagte and Ladysmith, and the King's South Africa Medal with clasps for South Africa 1901 and South Africa 1902. In 1902 he was commandant at a concentration camp at Middelburg, and in 1903 he was a district commissioner in the Eastern Transvaal.

In 1911 Johnston returned to Ireland and joined the General Prisons Board for Ireland. He was commandant of the POW camp at Oldcastle, County Meath, 1914–15, and was appointed governor of His Majesty's Convict Prison at Maryborough, County Laois in 1915, before returning to Oldcastle in 1916. He became a resident magistrate in 1918 and had a long career in the prison service.

Robert Johnston died on 24 March 1950 (although some sources say 1970) and is buried in St Mary's churchyard, Inistiogne, County Kilkenny. His VC is said to he displayed at the Light Horse Bar, Calcutta, India, but this remains unconfirmed.

Charles Herbert MULLINS, Elandslaagte, 21 October 1899

Charles Mullins was born on 28 June 1869 in Grahamstown, South Africa, the son of the Reverend Robert John Mullins. Educated at St Andrew's College, Grahamstown, and at Keble College, Oxford, he was called to the Bar at the Inner Temple in 1893. At some time prior to the Boer War Mullins enlisted into the Imperial Light Horse and reached the rank of captain.

In October 1899 the Boers captured Elandslaagte Station, thus cutting off Ladysmith. Lieutenant General Sir George White sent his cavalry commander, Major General John French, to recapture the

Charles Mullins.

station. Arriving shortly after dawn on the 21st, they found the Boers in some strength, with two field guns. French called up re-enforcements, which quickly arrived by train. British artillery bombarded the Boer position before assaulting it and the Imperial Light Horse charged on foot. At a most critical moment the advance was met with such a terrific fire that the men wavered for an instant. Mullins, with Captain Johnston, rushed forward through a hail of bullets and rallied the men, thus enabling the flanking movement to succeed. Both men were wounded during this action and were mentioned in despatches. Their VCs were gazetted on 12 February 1901.

Mullins was wounded again at Maritsani on 13 May 1900 and was medically discharged from the Imperial Light Horse with the rank of major. He arrived in England in 1901 and was presented with his VC, together with Johnston, by Edward VII on 25 July 1901. He was also awarded the Queen's South Africa Medal with clasps for Elandslaagte and Ladysmith, the King's South Africa Medal with clasps for South Africa 1901, and the CMG.

In 1902 Mullins married Norah Gertrude and they had two sons. He resumed his career in law but his war wounds left him crippled and he never fully recovered. He died on 24 May 1916 and is buried in Grahamstown Old Cemetery, South Africa.

His medals passed to his oldest son, and upon his death in 1963 they were left to St Andrew's College, Grahamstown. Years later, a family member went to the college to view the medals only to find they were not on display and missing. A search of the college discovered the VC but his other medals have never been found. As a consequence the medal was purchased in 1998 and it was passed to Charles Mullins's only grandson, but in 2005 it went on loan to the Imperial War Museum, London, where it is now on display in the Ashcroft Gallery.

Matthew Fontaine Maury MEIKLEJOHN, Elandslaagte, 21 October 1899

Matthew Meiklejohn was born on 27 November 1870 in Clapham, London, the son of John Meiklejohn, professor at the University of St Andrews. He was named after Matthew Fontaine Maury (1806–73), an American naval officer and hydrographer, and was educated at Madras College, Fife, and Fettes College, Edinburgh.

Meiklejohn joined the Gordon Highlanders while in India in June 1891, and in 1895 saw his first active service when Sir Robert Low took a Field Force to the relief of Chitral, by way of the Swat Valley, in what is now Pakistan. Two years later and the Gordons were in action again on the Indian Frontier, Meiklejohn being slightly wounded when his regiment charged the Dargai Heights. He also took part in the Tirah Expedition in 1897–98, seeing action in the Bara Valley. Meiklejohn received the India Medal with three clasps.

Matthew Meiklejohn.

On the outbreak of the Second Boer War, the Gordons were sent to South Africa with part of the infantry brigade from India. In October 1899, the Boers captured Elandslaagte Station, thus cutting off Ladysmith. Lieutenant General Sir George White sent his cavalry commander, Major General John French, to recapture the station. Arriving shortly after dawn on the 21st, they found the Boers in some strength, with two field guns. French called up re-enforcements, which quickly arrived by train. British artillery bombarded the Boer position, after which the assault went in, and the main Boer position had been taken. The Gordons were about to charge a kopje, but were exposed to a heavy crossfire and, having lost some officers, started to waver. Seeing the danger, Meiklejohn sprang forward, calling on the men to follow him. The position was captured, but he was severely wounded in four places and his right arm had to be amputated.

For this action he was awarded the VC, gazetted on 20 July 1900, by Queen Victoria on 15 December 1900. He was one of the last five to be given the award by Her Majesty. In 1901 he was appointed Garrison Adjutant at St Helena, where he returned to enter the Staff College. In 1904 he married Vera Marshall, daughter of the late Lieutenant Colonel Lionel Marshall, and they had a son and two daughters. While on the General Staff at army headquarters, Meiklejohn was promoted to major.

On 4 July 1913, Meiklejohn was riding in Hyde Park when his horse bolted and, due to the loss of his arm, he struggled to control the animal as it careered towards a group of children and their nursemaid. Meiklejohn managed to steer the animal into the railings bordering Rotten Row, throwing himself off but saving the children from serious injury or death. He died in hospital later the same day. Matthew Meiklejohn is buried in Brookwood Cemetery, St Judes Avenue, Plot 3, Grave 172317, Cemetery Pales, Woking, Surrey. His VC is held by the Gordon Highlanders Museum, Aberdeen.

Meiklejohn's grave, Brookwood Cemetery, Woking, Surrey.

William ROBERTSON, Elandslaagte, 21 October 1899

William Robertson was born on 27 February 1865 in Dumfries, the son of John and Janet Robertson. He was educated in Dumfries and joined the Gordon Highlanders on 1 December 1884. Robertson married Sara Ferris in 1891 and they had four children, William J. (born 1892, later a captain in the Royal Army Medical Corps), Marion M. (born 1895), Ian Gordon (born 1897, later a second lieutenant in the Gordon Highlanders and was killed in action on the Somme), and Hector E. (who became a Freemason in 1895).

William Robertson.

Robertson served four years in India before sailing to South Africa, arriving there on 8 October 1899 (just two days before the Boer ultimatum to Britain), and proceeded to Ladysmith. In October 1899 the Boers captured Elandslaagte Station, thus cutting off Ladysmith. Lieutenant General Sir George White sent his cavalry commander, Major General John French, to recapture the station. Arriving shortly after dawn on the 21st, they found the Boers in some strength, with two field guns. French called up re-enforcements, which quickly arrived by train. British artillery bombarded the Boer position, after which the assault went in, and during the final advance on the enemy's position Robertson led each successive rush. Once the main position had been taken, he led a party of men to seize the Boer camp. He then held this position under heavy fire, even after he was severely wounded.

For his action Robertson was awarded the VC, gazetted on 20 July 1900. He returned to England due to his wounds and received the award from Queen Victoria on 25 August 1900. He was awarded the Queen's South Africa Medal with clasps for Ladysmith, Elandslaagte and Cape Colony. Robertson was also awarded the Freedom of the Royal Burgh of Dumfries.

Robertson volunteered for service in the First World War but was turned down for a combat role due to his age. He was, however, employed as a recruiting officer in Edinburgh, with the rank of lieutenant colonel. He was also awarded the OBE. He retired in 1920 and became honorary treasurer of the Royal British Legion in Scotland, where he was known for his work on behalf of disabled ex-servicemen.

William Robertson died on 6 December 1949 and is buried in Portobello Cemetery (grave number is not recorded in the register), Edinburgh Road, Musselburgh, Lothian. Robertson's VC is held by the National War Museum of Scotland, Edinburgh Castle.

John NORWOOD, Ladysmith, 30 October 1899

John Norwood.

John Norwood was born on 8 September 1876 in Beckenham, Kent, the son of John Norwood of Pembury Lodge. He was educated at Abby School in Beckenham, and at Rugby School and Oxford University, before enlisting into the 5th (Princess of Wales) Dragoon Guards under the command of Lieutenant Colonel Baden-Powell in February 1899, just prior to the start of the Anglo-Boer War.

On 30 October 1899, Norwood went out from Ladysmith in charge of a small patrol. They came under such heavy fire from the enemy that when they had got to about 600 yards from them, the patrol had to retire at full speed. One man dropped and Norwood galloped back through heavy fire, dismounted, picked up the fallen trooper, and carried him on his back, at the same time leading his horse with one hand. All the time the enemy kept up an incessant fire on them.

For this action Norwood was awarded the VC, gazetted on 27 July 1900 and bestowed by the Commander-in-Chief, South Africa, Lord Frederick Sleigh Roberts VC on 25 October 1900 in Pretoria. Norwood also served in the Transvaal and the Orange River Colony, and was promoted to lieutenant in June 1900. He remained with his unit in South Africa until the war ended in May 1902, and left for Calcutta on the SS *Umlazi* two months later. He was promoted to captain in the 5th Dragoon Guards and joined the Reserve of Officers in February 1911.

At the start of the First World War Norwood joined the 2nd County of London Yeomanry, attached to the 5th Dragoon Guards, becoming part of the BEF. He was killed in action at the First Battle of the Marne at Sablonnières on 8 September (his birthday!) 1914, the first VC to be killed in action during the Great War. John Norwood is buried in Sablonnières New Communal Cemetery Extension, Plot 4, France. His VC is on loan to the Ashcroft Gallery, Imperial War Museum, London.

Norwood's grave, Sablonnières New Communal Cemetery Extension, France.

Horace Robert MARTINEAU, Game Tree Fort, 26 December 1899

Horace Martineau was born on 31 October 1874 in Bayswater, London, the fifth son of William Martineau. He was educated at University College School, London, before enlisting into the 11th Hussars in 1891 and was garrisoned at Pietermaritzburg. In 1982 he served at Rawalpindi, India, before purchasing his discharge in 1895, when he returned to South Africa. In 1896 he served under Sir Robert Baden-Powell in the successful campaign against the Matabele.

Martineau served in the Cape Police but, on the outbreak of the Boer War, he joined the Protectorate Regiment (North Cape Colony). On 26 December 1899, Baden-Powell launched an attack on the Boer positions on Game Tree Hill, near Mafeking; the Boers were expecting the attack and had strengthened their position. When the retreat had been sounded Martineau remained

Horace Martineau.

behind to assist Corporal Le Camp, who was lying wounded 10 yards from the Boer trenches. Half dragging and half carrying Le Camp to cover under a bush, where he attended to his wounds, Martineau was himself wounded three times and was forced to give up. As a result of his wounds his left arm was amputated.

For this action he was awarded the VC, gazetted on 6 July 1900, and was presented with it by Lord Roberts VC on 11 December 1900 in Cape Town. Martineau played no further part in the war and took up employment with the government offices in Cape Town. Then, in 1906, he served in the Bambatha Rebellion, before working for the African Boating Company. He married Raymond Harman, and they had a daughter.

During the First World War Martineau served in the transport service at Suez and Gallipoli, where he contracted a fever and was sent back to Egypt. After recovery he became involved in an altercation with a Captain Hunt, during which Martineau used insubordinate language. The commandant of Base Headquarters at Alexandria recommended that as he was a recipient of the VC, 'his service be dispensed with without trial and that he be sent back to New Zealand'. While waiting for a decision on his future, Martineau became ill and was admitted to hospital with colitis. On 29 November 1915, he returned to New Zealand on the hospital ship *Maheno*, arriving on New Year's Day 1916. On 24 February that year, Martineau was struck off the strength of the New Zealand Expeditionary Force, an ignominious end for a military hero whose enlistment had been so proudly publicised.

Horace Martineau died from gastritis and haematemesis (vomiting of blood due to prolonged erosion of the stomach lining) on 7 April 1916 and is buried in Andersons Bay Soldiers' Cemetery, Returned Serviceman's Area, Block 73, Plot 16, Dunedin, New Zealand. He is also named on the family grave in Brookwood Cemetery, Woking, Surrey. His VC is in the Ashcroft Gallery, Imperial War Museum, London.

Horace Edward RAMSDEN, Game Tree Fort, 26 December 1899

Horace Ramsden was born on 15 December 1878 in Chester, a descendant of Sir John Ramsden. His family emigrated to South Africa in 1891 and Horace attended school in Cape Town. At 17 he enlisted into the Prince

Alfred's Own Cape Artillery and served in the Bechuanaland Rebellion. At the outbreak of the Boer War Ramsden joined the Protectorate Regiment and reluctantly smuggled his younger brother Alfred onto the train to serve with him. They were present at the relief of Ladysmith.

Then, on 26 December 1899, when in action at Game Tree Fort, after the retreat was sounded he remained behind to assist his brother, who had been shot through both legs and was lying 10 yards from the Boer trenches. He carried him 600–800 yards under heavy fire, putting him down from time to time to rest until help arrived and he was taken to a place of safety. This was the second VC awarded for saving the life of a brother, the first being to Hugh Gough VC during the Indian Mutiny of 1857.

Horace Ramsden.

Ramsden's VC was gazetted on 6 July 1900 and he was presented with it on 28 October that year by Lord Roberts VC at Pretoria. Promoted to lieutenant, he was transferred to Lord Roberts's bodyguard and after the war he obtained a commission in the Johannesburg Mounted Rifles. He married Ade Tomlinson, a widow, and they had a son.

During the First World War Ramsden served with Hartigan's Horse in South Africa, where he was taken prisoner by the Germans. After the war he was released and he remained in South Africa.

Horace Ramsden died on 3 August 1948 and he was cremated at Maitland Crematorium, Woltemade, Cape Town. His ashes were removed by the undertaker and presumably given to the family. His VC is now in the Ashcroft Gallery, Imperial War Museum, London.

Chapter 8

Magersfontein and Colenso

Henry Edward Manning DOUGLAS, Magersfontein, 11 December 1899

Henry Douglas was born on 11 July 1875 in Brompton Convict Prison, Gillingham, Kent, where his father was a warder. He was one of nine children of George and Elizabeth Douglas. After being educated in Edinburgh, he took the Scottish Triple Qualification in 1898 and was commissioned a lieutenant in the Royal Army Medical Corps on 28 July 1899. He travelled to South Africa following the outbreak of the Boer War.

Henry Douglas.

On 11 December 1899, British forces attempted to relieve the mining town of Kimberly. It was here that Douglas, who was wounded in the face by a bullet, advanced into the open to attend to the wounds of Major Robinson and Captian Gordon (who would himself be awarded the VC for action at Krugersdorp) under very heavy fire. He performed many similar acts of gallantry on the same day. For this act he was mentioned in despatches and awarded the VC, gazetted on 29 March 1901.

Douglas was invalided home due to his wound but was back in South Africa just two months later. He returned home again in early 1900 and was presented with his VC on 25 July 1901 by the King at St James's Palace, London. He was promoted to captain before leaving for service in Somaliland in 1903, and was present at the Battle of Jidballi. In 1906 he served at Army HQ and the following year was stationed in Lucknow.

After this he took time off from military duties and was part of Robert Sterling Clark's sixteen-month expedition to North China. On his return he was a resident at the Royal Army Medical College in Westminster, being promoted to major in 1911, and 1912–13 saw Douglas taking part in the First Balkan War. He also served in the First World War, ending with the rank of brevet colonel in 1918.

From 1926 to 1929, Douglas was a consultant at the Royal Army Medical College in Milbank and during this time he was made a full colonel. Three years later, he was again promoted, this time to major general, and became Deputy Director of Medical Services at Southern Command, India.

Henry Douglas retired from the army in 1933 and died on 14 February 1939. He is buried in Epsom Cemetery, Section H, Grave 132, Ashley Road, Epsom, Surrey. His VC is held by the Museum of Military Medicine, Keogh Barracks, Aldershot, Surrey.

Douglas's grave, Epsom Cemetery, Surrey.

John David Francis SHAUL, Magersfontein, 11 December 1899

John Shaul was born on 11 September 1873 in King's Lynn, Norfolk, the son of Sergeant John Shaul, a Crimea and China veteran. He was educated at the Duke of York's School, Chelsea. At 15 he joined the Highland Light Infantry and served in Crete during the fighting in 1897–98.

On 10 December 1899, British forces intended to clear a way through the lines of Magersfontein. The Highland Brigade advanced in massed column to prevent loss of formation during the hours of darkness. The

John Shaul.

order to extend had just been given when deadly fire from the Boers was poured into them. The head and flank of the column broke under the murderous fire; they dropped dead and wounded in their hundreds. The battle raged all night and into the next day when the Boer artillery, which had remained silent, suddenly opened fire, adding their deadly fire upon the British cavalry. The British withdrew out of range, leaving nearly a thousand dead and wounded. Shaul, although in charge of the stretcher-bearers, was seen to encourage the men forward during the first day of the action. On the following day he went from one man to another, dressing their wounds, and in one case he came, under a terrific fire, to a man wounded in the back; with utter coolness he sat down beside him and dressed his wounds. Having done this, he got up and went quietly to another part of the field. Shaul carried out this act as if there had been no enemy nearby.

Shaul was presented with his VC on 11 August 1901 by the Duke of Cornwall & York (the future King George V) at Pietermaritzburg. In 1904 he was stationed in Khartoum and he left his battalion in Lucknow, India, after twenty-one years' service. He moved to South Africa and worked for the East Rand Premier gold mine in Boksburg. He was bandmaster of the Imperial Light Horse and served in the First World War with the 5th South African Infantry in East Africa, later being invalided home with dysentery.

John Shaul died on 14 September 1953 and is buried in Old Cemetery, Boksburg, South Africa. His VC is in the Ashcroft Gallery, Imperial War Museum, London.

Ernest Beachcroft Beckwith TOWSE, Magersfontein and Mount Thada, 11 December 1899 & 30 April 1900

Ernest Towse was born on 23 April 1864 in Westminster, London, and was educated at Wellington College. He joined the Gordon Highlanders in 1886 and married Gertrude Christie in 1892, younger daughter of John Christie. He served with the Chitral Relief Force in 1895, on the North-West Frontier of India, and in the Tirah Expedition in 1897–98.

On 10 December 1899, British forces intended to clear a way through the lines of Magersfontein. The Highland Brigade advanced in massed column to prevent loss of formation during the hours of darkness. The order to extend had just been given when deadly fire from the Boers was poured into them. The head and flank of the column broke under the murderous fire; they dropped dead and wounded in their hundreds. The battle raged all night and into the next day, when Colonel Downman was mortally wounded. Towse tried to carry him on his back but finding him impossible to lift, he remained with him in the firing line until assistance arrived. He was mentioned in Lord Methuen's despatches.

Ernest Towse.

Then, on 30 April 1900, in one of the most dramatic fights of the Boer War, Towse and a party of twelve men from the Gordons and Kitchener's Horse confronted 150 Boers and were called on to surrender, but he ordered his men to open fire and remained firing himself until the Boers were driven back in utter confusion. Towse was wounded in both eyes, leaving him blinded for the rest of his life.

Towse was decorated with the VC in July 1900 by the Queen at Windsor Castle. It is said that she shed tears when pinning the VC on him. Probably at her insistence, the War Office awarded Towse a special wounds pension of £300 a year. The Queen also appointed him sergeant-at-arms. Edward VII reappointed him in 1902, and in 1903 he

Towse's grave, St Thomas of Canterbury churchyard, Goring-on-Thames, Oxfordshire.

was admitted to the Honorary Corps of Gentleman-at-Arms, in which he served until 1939.

At the outbreak of the First World War, Towse offered his service as a typist, writing letters for wounded soldiers at the front. He was promoted to staff captain of Base Hospitals without pay and allowances, and was mentioned in despatches in 1916. He became chairman of the Grand Council of the Comrades of the Great War and in 1921 accompanied Field Marshal Haig to South Africa to form an Empire League of ex-servicemen.

Ernest Towse died on 21 June 1948 and is buried in St Thomas of Canterbury churchyard, Goring-on-Thames, Oxfordshire. His VC is held by the Gordon Highlanders Museum, Aberdeen.

Walter Norris 'Squibs' CONGREVE, Colenso, 15 December 1899

Walter Congreve was born on 20 November 1862 in Chatham, Kent, the son of William Congreve JP and Fanny Emma (née Townsend). He is related to Sir William Congreve, who developed the Congreve rocket, used during the Napoleonic Wars. He was educated at Harrow School and Oxford University but failed to graduate, due to an unfortunate incident involving the wounding of a senior member of the college with an air rifle. Congreve joined the Rifle Brigade (Prince Consort's Own) in 1855; he served in the 3rd Burma War in 1885 and was promoted to captain in 1893.

Walter Congreve.

On 15 December 1899, Sir Redvers Buller VC led an advance on the Boer positions at the Tugela River, near Colenso, with five infantry brigades and artillery support, numbering 21,000 men. This was to be the first step in the relief of Ladysmith, which had been under siege since 2 November that year. The attack was frontal and three-pronged: both flanks were repulsed; on the right the artillery had been brought too far forward and many of the gunners and limber horses became casualties.

Congreve, with Captain Harry Schofield, Lieutenant Frederick Roberts, Corporal George Nurse and Private George Ravenhill, tried to save the guns of the 14th and 66th batteries; some of the horses and drivers were sheltering in a donga about 500 yards behind the guns and the ground between them was swept with rifle and shellfire. Under heavy fire, Congreve, Schofield, Roberts, Nurse and Ravenhill helped to hook up a team of horses and limber up a gun, and then Nurse managed on his own to limber up a second gun. Congreve, despite being wounded himself, helped bring back the mortally wounded Lieutenant Roberts, with the assistance of Major William Babtie. Congreve was shot though the leg, through the toe of his boot, was grazed on the elbow and shoulder, and his horse was shot in three places.

His VC was gazetted on 2 February 1900, and he was presented with it on 25 October that year at Pretoria by Lord Roberts VC, the father of the man he tried in vain to save. He then served as Private Secretary to Lord Kitchener in South Africa. In 1900 he married Celia La Touche and they had three sons. Congreve was promoted to major and then in 1901 to lieutenant colonel, and was appointed Assistant Military Secretary and ADC to HRH the Duke of Connaught in Ireland. Congreve was appointed commandant of the School of Musketry in 1909, where he greatly improved rifle skills, raising the rate of fire to fifteen aimed rounds a minute. He was promoted to major general in 1915 and served throughout the First World War, where he lost a hand (the only corps commander to be wounded during the war), and in Palestine. Congreve was not an unqualified success as a corps commander. Haig was known to question his efficiency. However, during the July offensive on the Somme his two divisions were the only ones to take all their objectives, earning Haig's grudging congratulations. His tactics during the 1918 German offensive proved disastrous and he was removed from command, Haig refusing to see him.

Walter Congreve was appointed Governor of Malta, and it was there that he died from heart disease on 28 February 1927. He was buried at sea (at his own request), off the coast of Malta, in the Mediterranean. His VC is held by the Royal Green Jackets Museum, Winchester, Hampshire. His son William was also awarded the VC during the First World War, making them one of only three pairs of father and son VCs.

George Edward NURSE, Colenso, 15 December 1899

George Nurse was born on 14 April 1873 in Enniskillen, County Fermanagh, Northern Ireland, the son of Charles and Jane Nurse. He was educated at the Chamberlain Academy, Guernsey, and joined the Royal Artillery in London in 1892. He went to South Africa in early 1899 at the outbreak of the Boer War.

On 15 December 1899, Sir Redvers Buller VC led an advance on the Boer positions at the Tugela River, near Colenso, with five infantry brigades and artillery support, numbering 21,000 men. This was to be the first step in the relief of Ladysmith, which had been under siege since 2 November that year. The attack was frontal and three-pronged, and both flanks were repulsed; on the left the artillery had been brought too far forward and many of the gunners and limber horses became casualties.

George Nurse.

Nurse, with Captain Harry Schofield, Captain Walter Congreve, Lieutenant Frederick Roberts and Private George Ravenhill, tried to save the guns of the 14th and 66th batteries; some of the horses and drivers were sheltering in a donga about 500 yards behind the guns and the ground between them was swept with rifle and shellfire. Congreve, Schofield, Roberts, Nurse and Ravenhill, under heavy fire, helped to hook up a team of horses and limber up a gun, and then Nurse managed on his own to limber up a second gun.

Nurse's VC was gazetted on 4 March 1900 and it was presented to him that same month by Sir Redvers Buller VC at Ladysmith. He served throughout the remainder of the war before returning to England. Later, he served as a temporary second lieutenant during the First World War. He had a son, whom he named Charles T. Colenso Nurse.

Nurse's grave, Allerton Cemetery, Liverpool.

George Nurse died on 25 November 1945. He is buried in Allerton Cemetery, C of E Section 2-G, Grave 608, Woolton Road, Liverpool, Merseyside. His VC is held by the Royal Artillery Museum (in storage), Larkhill, Wiltshire.

George Albert RAVENHILL, Colenso, 15 December 1899

George Ravenhill was born on 21 February 1872 in Birmingham, one of nine children to Thomas and Anne Ravenhill. He enlisted into the Royal Scots Fusiliers in May 1889 and spent six years in India. Ravenhill married Florence Langford in 1898 and their first child was born the following year.

George Ravenhill.

On 15 December 1899, Sir Redvers Buller VC led an advance on the Boer positions at the Tugela River, near Colenso, with five infantry brigades and artillery support, numbering 21,000 men. This was to be the first step in the relief of Ladysmith, which had been under siege since 2 November that year. The attack was frontal and three-pronged and both flanks were repulsed. On the left the artillery had been brought too far forward and many of the gunners and limber horses became casualties.

Private Ravenhill, with Captain Harry Schofield, Captain Walter Congreve, Lieutenant Frederick Roberts and Corporal George Nurse, tried to save the guns of the 14th and 66th batteries. Some of the horses and drivers were sheltering in a donga about 500 yards behind the guns and the ground between them was swept with rifle and shellfire. Congreve, Schofield, Roberts, Nurse and Ravenhill, under heavy fire, helped to hook up a team of horses and limber up a gun, and then Nurse managed on his own to limber up a second gun. During the action, Ravenhill was injured, being shot through the forearm.

Ravenhill's VC was gazetted on 4 June 1901 and he was presented with it by the Duke of Cornwall & York (later George V) at Pietermaritzburg on 14 August 1901. Ravenhill left the army in 1908 after thirteen years' service. Unfortunately, his life took a turn for the worse as he fell on hard times. His case was even mentioned in the House of Commons in May when Mr C.B. Harmsworth MP asked the Secretary of State for War if anything could be done to help him. The response was that the case was still under investigation.

No action was taken later that year when he fell foul of the law. He had already been to court charged with not performing his duties at the Erdington Workhouse, when in August 1908 he was charged with the theft of iron to the value of six shillings. His defence was that he believed he was entitled to a pension of £50 a year but had heard nothing about his claim. The judge did not agree and Ravenhill was imprisoned for a month as he was unable to pay the ten shilling fine.

Due to his conviction Ravenhill was the subject of a forfeiture warrant signed by the sovereign, meaning his medal was to be returned. However, he was not struck off the Register of the Victoria Cross as only the medal was forfeited.

The practice was discontinued in 1920 when George V was so concerned by the prospect of future forfeits it was declared: 'The King feels so strongly that, no matter the crime committed by anyone on whom the VC has been conferred, the decoration should not be forfeited. Even were a VC [holder] be sentenced to be hanged for murder, he should be allowed to wear his VC on the scaffold.'

After Ravenhill's release from prison things only got worse; three of his four children were sent to the USA and Canada for adoption. Two more children were born, in 1910 and 1911, but both died in infancy. He served on the home front during the First World War.

George Ravenhill died from a heart attack on 14 April 1921 and is buried in Witton Cemetery, Section 47, Plot 36, Grave 08654, Moor Lane, Witton, Birmingham. His VC is held by the Royal Highland Fusiliers Museum, Glasgow.

Ravenhill's grave, Witton Cemetery, Birmingham.

Frederick Hugh Sherston ROBERTS, Colenso, 15 December 1899

Frederick Roberts.

Frederick Roberts was born on 8 January 1872 in Umballa, India, the son of Field Marshal Lord 'Bobs' Roberts VC (one of only three pairs of father and son VCs) and Nora Henrietta (née Bews). He was educated at Eton College and joined the army soon after completing his studies, and then served for four years in India. In 1897–98 he was ADC to Major General Sir Herbert Kitchener in the Nile Expeditionary Force.

On 15 December 1899, Sir Redvers Buller VC led an advance on the Boer positions the Tugela River, near Colenso, with five infantry brigades and artillery support, numbering 21,000 men. This was to be the first step in the relief of Ladysmith, which had been under siege since 2 November that year. The attack was frontal and three-pronged, and both flanks were repulsed. On the left the artillery had been brought too far forward and many of the gunners and limber horses became casualties.

Lieutenant Roberts, with Captain Harry Schofield, Captain Walter Congreve, Corporal George Nurse and Private George Ravenhill, tried to save the guns of the 14th and 66th batteries. Some of the horses and drivers were sheltering in a donga about 500 yards behind the guns and the ground between them was swept with rifle and shellfire. Congreve, Schofield, Roberts, Nurse and Ravenhill, under heavy fire, helped to hook up a team of horses and limber up a gun, and then Nurse managed on his own to limber up a second gun. Roberts was mortally wounded during this action and was helped back by Captain Walter Congreve and Major William Babtie. Roberts died two days later.

The action was witnessed by the C-in-C Redvers Buller VC, who, under rule seven of the Victoria Cross Warrant, could have conferred the award on the spot but instead recommended Roberts in his despatch dated 16 December, the day before he died of his wounds.

Because the recommendation was dated before Roberts's death it was approved, partly due to his family connections with the Queen (his father being Victoria's favourite soldier), thus ending the unwritten rule on only awarding the medal to those who survived. Later, two batches of six VCs were backdated to others who would have been awarded it had they survived their VC action. This is the only time the VC has been awarded retrospectively.

Frederick Roberts is buried in Chievely War Cemetery, Plot 136, Frere, South Africa. His VC is held by the National Army Museum, London.

Harry Norton SCHOFIELD, Colenso, 15 December 1899

Harry Schofield was born on 29 January 1865 in Audenshaw, Manchester, the son of Christopher Schofield JP. He attended the Royal Military Academy at Woolwich. Commissioned into the Royal Artillery in 1884, he was promoted to captain in 1893.

On 15 December 1899, Sir Redvers Buller VC led an advance on the Boer positions at the Tugela River, near Colenso, with five infantry brigades and artillery support, numbering 21,000 men. This was to be the first step in the relief of Ladysmith, which had been under siege since 2 November that year. The attack was frontal and three-pronged, and both flanks were repulsed. On the left the artillery had been brought too far forward and many of the gunners and limber horses became casualties.

Harry Schofield.

Captain Schofield, with Captain Walter Congreve, Lieutenant Frederick Roberts, Corporal George Nurse and Private George Ravenhill, tried to save the guns of the 14th and 66th batteries. Some of the horses and drivers were sheltering in a donga about 500 yards behind the guns and the ground between them was swept with rifle and shellfire. Congreve, Schofield, Roberts, Nurse and Ravenhill, under heavy fire, helped to hook up a team of horses and then limber up a gun, and then Nurse managed on his own to limber up a second gun.

Schofield also saw action at Spion Kop, Vaal Krantz, Pieter's Hill, the relief of Ladysmith and Laing's Nek, and in the Eastern Transvaal at Belfast and Lydenburg. He was mentioned in despatches four times and was awarded the DSO for his action at Colenso (gazetted on 19 April 1900) because Buller would not recommend him for the VC as he had been ordered to help save the guns, but it was later decided he could be awarded the VC for an action even if so ordered. The DSO was cancelled and the VC awarded, gazetted on 30 August 1901 and presented by Edward VII on 29 October 1901.

Schofield's grave, Putney Vale Cemetery, London.

In 1905 Schofield left the army and became a member of His Majesty's Honourable Corps of Gentlemen-At-Arms. He also served throughout the First World War. He died on 10 October 1931, following a long illness, and is buried in Putney Vale Cemetery, Block L, Grave 29, Stag Lane, London. His VC is in the Ashcroft Gallery, Imperial War Museum, London.

William BABTIE, Colenso, 15 December 1899

William Babtie was born on 7 May 1859 in Dumbarton, Scotland, the eldest son of John Babtie JP. He was educated at the University of Glasgow and took up his degree in 1880, entering the Army Medical Services the following year. He served during the international occupation of Crete in 1897–98.

On 15 December 1899, Sir Redvers Buller VC led an advance on the Boer positions at the Tugela River, near Colenso, with five infantry brigades and artillery support, numbering 21,000 men. This was to be the first step in the relief of Ladysmith, which had been under siege since 2 November that year. The attack was frontal and three-pronged, and both flanks were repulsed. On the left the artillery had been brought too far forward and many of the gunners and limber horses became casualties.

A message was sent back asking for assistance. Babtie rode up under heavy fire to attend to the wounded, who were lying in a donga close to the guns. He was exposed to heavy fire while dressing their wounds. Later the same day he went to bring in, under a heavy fire, the mortally wounded Lieutenant Frederick Roberts, with the help of Walter Congreve.

William Babtie.

Babtie was presented with his VC, gazetted on 20 April 1900, by Lord Roberts in Pretoria on 25 October 1900. From 1901 to 1906 he was Assistant Director General Army Medical Services, War Office. In 1903, Babtie married Edith Barry and they had a daughter. From 1907 to 1910, he was Inspector of Medical Services, and from 1910 to 1914, Deputy Director General.

During the First World War, Babtie served as Director of Medical Services in India from 1914 to 1915, and as principal Director of Medical Services in the Mediterranean during operations in Egypt, the Dardanelles and Salonika in 1915 to 1916, and was mentioned in despatches. In 1916 he became Director and in 1918 Inspector of Medical Services at the War Office.

William Babtie died in Knokke, Belgium, on 11 September 1920, and is buried in Stoke (Old) Cemetery, Stoughton Road, Guildford, Surrey. His VC is held by the Museum of Military Medicine, Keogh Barracks, Aldershot, Surrey.

Babtie's grave, Stoke (Old) Cemetery, Guildford, Surrey.

Hamilton Lyster REED, Colenso, 15 December 1899

Hamilton Reed was born on 23 May 1869 in Dublin, Ireland, the son of Sir Andrew Reed, Inspector General, Royal Irish Constabulary. He was educated at the Royal Military Academy, Woolwich, and joined the Royal Field Artillery in February 1888, being promoted to captain the following year.

On 15 December 1899, Sir Redvers Buller VC led an advance on the Boer positions at the Tugela River, near Colenso, with five infantry brigades and artillery support, numbering 21,000 men. This was to be the first step in the relief of Ladysmith, which had been under siege since 2 November that year. The attack was frontal and three-pronged, and both flanks were repulsed. On the left the artillery had been brought too far forward and many of the gunners and limber horses became casualties.

Hamilton Reed.

After two guns had been recovered by others, Reed brought three teams of horses from his battery in an attempt to save the remaining guns of the 14th and 66th batteries. The rifle and shellfire was intense and he was wounded almost at once, as were five of the thirteen men who went with him. Another was killed, along with thirteen of the horses, before they got halfway to the guns and they were forced to retire.

Reed's VC was gazetted on 2 February 1900 and he was presented with it at Ladysmith on 4 March 1900. He then saw action at Spion Kop, Vaal Krantz and at the Tugela Heights. From March

Reed's grave, Richmond Cemetery, Richmond-upon-Thames, Surrey.

to June 1900 he was in action in Natal and Laing's Nek, and later in the Transvaal at Belfast and Lydenburg. From 1900 to 1902, he served in the Orange River Colony.

Promoted to major in 1904, Reed passed the Staff College exam in 1905 and was on the General Staff at Army Headquarters 1906–10. In 1911 he married Marjorie Eleanor and they had a son and two daughters. Reed was then Military Attaché with the Turkish Army 1912–13 during the Balkan War. He also served in the First World War, being mentioned in despatches seven times.

Hamilton Reed died on 7 March 1931 and is buried in Richmond Cemetery, Section E, Grave 210, Lower Grove Road, Richmond-upon-Thames, Surrey.

Chapter 9

Colesberg and Relief of Ladysmith

John Peniston MILBANKE, Colesberg, 5 January 1900

John Milbanke was born on 9 October 1872 in London, the son of Peniston Milbanke, 9th Baronet, JP, Deputy Lieutenant of Sussex. He was educated at Castlemount School, Dover, and Harrow, where he became a close friend of Winston Churchill. Milbanke enlisted into the 10th Hussars in November 1892, and succeeded his father as the 10th Baronet in 1899.

In South Africa he served as ADC to General French. On 5 January 1900, while on a reconnaissance near Colesberg with three men, as they were retiring under fire and notwithstanding the fact that Milbanke had been severely wounded in the thigh, he rode back under heavy fire to one of his men whose horse was exhausted and took the man onto his own horse and carried him back to camp.

John Milbanke.

Milbanke was mentioned in despatches and his VC was gazetted on 6 July 1900. He was presented with it by the Queen at Windsor Castle on 15 December the same year. He was one of the last five to be given the award by her. In December 1901 he married Leila, only daughter of Colonel the Hon. Charles Crichton, and they had two sons. Milbanke retired from the army in 1910 but on the outbreak of the First World War he re-enlisted, taking command of the Nottingham Yeomanry (Sherwood Foresters), and went to Egypt in April 1915.

John Milbanke was killed in action at Suvla Bay, Gallipoli, on 21 August 1915 and has no known grave. His is named on the Hellas Memorial to the missing, Panel 16. His VC is held by the Royal Hussars Museum, Winchester, Hampshire.

Herman ALBRECHT, Ladysmith, 6 January 1900

Herman Albrecht was born in 1876 at Burgersdorf; he was orphaned and was raised by a Mr P. Shorten in the Burghersdorp-Aliwal North area of Cape Town, South Africa. He was an excellent sportsman and made his money driving post-carts and breaking in horses. At the outbreak of the Boer War he enlisted into the Imperial Light Horse (Natal).

Herman Albrecht.

On 6 January 1900, Albrecht and Lieutenant Robert Digby-Jones led the attack on Wagon Hill, near Ladysmith. They scrambled to the gun pits before the enemy could reach them. Once there, Digby-Jones shot the Boer leader Field Cornet Japie de Villiers and killed three more Boers with successive shots; he then killed another with the butt of his revolver before he himself was killed by a bullet to the throat. Meanwhile, Albrecht also killed at least two Boers before he too was shot dead. Their action prevented the Boers from capturing this critical position.

Herman Albrecht is buried in a mass grave, Wagon Hill Cemetery, Ladysmith, in the KwaZulu-Natal region of South Africa. He is named on the Imperial Light Horse Memorial at the same location. On 8 August 1902, as a result of the award to Lieutenant Frederick Roberts, the policy in the War Office was changed and both men were gazetted the VC. Albrecht's VC is held by the Museum of Military History, Johannesburg, South Africa.

Robert James Thomas DIGBY-JONES, Ladysmith, 6 January 1900

Robert Digby-Jones was born on 27 September 1876 in Edinburgh, the son of Charles Digby-Jones and Aimee Susanna (née Christie). He was educated first at Alnmouth, Northumberland, and at Sedbergh School, and was known to be a good all-round athlete. Digby-Jones passed into the Royal Academy at Woolwich in 1894, being commissioned into the Royal Artillery two years later.

He was posted to South Africa in June 1899, serving at Ladysmith, where he was involved in the construction of a hospital in the camp. On 11 December 1899 he blew up a 4.7-inch howitzer on Surprise Hill, which had been causing heavy damage to the garrison with its 40lb shells.

On 6 January 1900, with Trooper Herman Albrecht, he led the attack on Wagon Hill, near Ladysmith. They scrambled to the gun

Robert Digby-Jones.

pits before the enemy could reach them. Once there, Digby-Jones shot the Boer leader 'De Villiers' and killed three more Boers with successive shots; he then killed another with the butt of his revolver before he was killed by a bullet to the throat. Meanwhile, Albrecht also killed at least two Boers before he too was shot dead. Their action prevented the Boers from capturing this critical position. The South African Review of 24 February declared that Digby-Jones 'saved Ladysmith and the British Army from defeat'.

Robert Digby-Jones is buried in Ladysmith Cemetery, in the KwaZulu-Natal region of South Africa. He is also named on the family grave in Dean Cemetery, Edinburgh. On 8 August 1902, as a result of the award to Lieutenant Frederick Roberts, the policy in the War Office was changed and both men were gazetted the VC. Digby-Jones's VC is held by the Royal Engineers Museum, Gillingham, Kent.

James Edward Ignatius MASTERSON, Ladysmith, 6 January 1900

James Masterson was born on 20 June 1862 in Birr, County Offaly, Ireland, and was educated by the Marist Brothers. His ancestor, Major Masterson, captured a Napoleonic eagle at Barossa in 1811 and was given a field commission (the incident was portrayed in an episode of *Sharpe*). James joined the Royal Fusiliers in 1881, and served in Egypt, taking part in the Battle of Tel-el-Kebir. He was commissioned second lieutenant in the 2nd Devonshire Regiment in July 1891 and served in Burma in 1891–92. He then served under Sir William Lockhart with the 1st Battalion in the Tirah Expedition 1897–98, on the North-West Frontier of India.

Sent to South Africa in late 1899, he was present at the Battle of Elandslaagte, and the actions at Rietfontein and Lombard's Kop. On 6 January 1900 he led his company in a successful charge at Wagon Hill, near Ladysmith. His men were then exposed to very heavy fire from both flanks, so he crossed an open plain under fire to request support from the Imperial Light Horse to fire to the left front and endeavour to check the enemy's fire. Despite being shot through both thighs, he crawled (a distance of 100 yards) and delivered the message before collapsing with exhaustion.

James Masterson.

Mentioned in despatches three times, his VC was gazetted on 4 June 1901 and he was presented with it on 6 September that year. He stayed in South Africa until the end of the war and in October 1902 sailed to India with his regiment. Masterson was promoted to major in 1911 but was placed on the retired list the following year. During the First World War he served as a transport officer, finally leaving the army in 1918.

James Masterson died on 24 December 1935 and is buried in Waterlooville Cemetery, Hulbert Road, Waterlooville, Hampshire. His VC is held by the Devonshire & Dorset Regiment Museum, The Keep, Dorchester, Dorset.

Masterson's grave, Waterlooville Cemetery, Hampshire.

James PITTS, Caesar's Camp, 6 January 1900

James Pitts was born on 26 February 1877 in Blackburn, Lancashire, the oldest of sixteen children to Patrick Pitts, an umbrella hawker. He was educated at St Ann's and then St Alban's schools. Pitts left school at 13 and was employed in a mill until he was 18, when he enlisted into the 1st Manchester Regiment. In November 1897 he sailed for Gibraltar, and two years later he was on his way to South Africa.

James Pitts.

On 6 January 1900, at Caesar's camp, east of Wagon Hill, sixteen men from 'D' Company were defending a sangar on the hillside. The men were under heavy fire all day, the majority being killed and their positions occupied by the enemy. At last only Privates Pitts and Scott remained. They held their post for fifteen hours without food or water, all the time exchanging fire with the enemy, until relief troops had retaken the lost ground and pushed the Boers off the hill.

Both men were gazetted for the VC on 26 July 1901 and presented with their medals together by the Commander-in-Chief South Africa, Lord Kitchener, on 8 June 1902 at Pretoria.

Pitts returned to Blackburn, where he was given a warm welcome and £50 from the mayor. He took up work as a labourer at the Bank Top Foundry, but found regular work hard to come by. In 1908 he was approached about selling his VC and refused, saying that 'he would rather suffer than part with it'. In 1914, Pitts re-enlisted, joining his old regiment, and served throughout the First World War. After the war he took up work for the Highways Department with Blackburn Corporation and remained there for thirty-four years.

Pitts's grave, Whalley New Road Cemetery, Blackburn, Lancashire.

James Pitts died on 18 February 1955 and was buried with full military honours in Whalley New Road Cemetery, RC Section, Plot D, Grave 2524, Whalley New Road, Blackburn, Lancashire. His VC is held by the Manchester Regiment Museum, Town Hall, Ashton-under-Lyne.

Robert SCOTT, Caesar's Camp, 6 January 1900

Robert Scott was born on 4 June 1874 in Haslingden, Lancashire, one of eight children of James Scott, a cotton operative. He was educated at Haslingden Parish Church day school and attended the New Jerusalem Sunday School. Robert worked at the Flash Mill Warehouse as a weaver for five years before enlisting into the 1st Manchester Regiment in 1895, and four years later was sent to South Africa.

On 6 January 1900, at Caesar's camp, east of Wagon Hill, sixteen men from 'D' Company were defending a sangar on the hillside. The men were under heavy fire all day, the majority being killed and their positions occupied by the enemy. At last only Private Scott, who had been shot through the ear, and Private Pitts remained. They held their post for fifteen hours without food or water, all the time exchanging fire with the enemy, until relief troops had retaken the lost ground and pushed the Boers off the hill. Both men were gazetted for the VC on 26 July 1901 and presented with their medals together by the Commander-in-Chief South Africa, Lord Kitchener, on 8 June 1902 at Pretoria.

Robert Scott.

Scott returned home to Haslingden in October 1902 to a hero's welcome. He left the army and married Alice Grimshaw and they had two daughters. He held a job with the Westinghouse engineering works at Trafford Park, then rejoined his regiment in 1904, and then became a schoolmaster. During the First World War he was an orderly sergeant at Ashton Barracks in Greater Manchester.

He left the army in 1923 and moved to Ireland, where he joined the Royal Irish Constabulary. He served with the RAF during the Second

World War and was awarded the DSM in 1929. After the war he worked in the Civil Service until his retirement.

Robert Scott died on 21 February 1961 and is buried in Christchurch Church of Ireland Cemetery, Newry Street, Kilkeel, Co Down, Northern Ireland. His VC was donated to the Manchester Regiment Museum, Town Hall, Ashton-under-Lyne, Greater Manchester.

Chapter 10

Paardeberg

Alfred ATKINSON, Paardeberg, 18 February 1900

Alfred Atkinson was born on 6 February 1874 in Leeds, Yorkshire, the son of Farrier Major James Atkinson who served in 'H' Battery, 4th Brigade, Royal Artillery. It is believed that it was this battery that captured the guns in the Crimea that the first VCs were made from (Note: not the medal from the 'Woolwich guns' which was first used in 1914). Alfred enlisted into the 1st Battalion, Yorkshire Regiment (later the Green Howards), then went on the Reserve list. He rejoined on the outbreak of the Boer War.

Alfred Atkinson.

On 18 February 1900, during the Battle of Paardeberg, Sergeant Atkinson carried water for the wounded. Seven times he went back and forth under a heavy and close fire. On the last trip he was shot in the head. He died on 21 February 1900 as a result of his wounds and is buried in an unmarked grave (exact location of grave unknown) in the Gruisbank British Cemetery, Paardeberg, in the Orange Free State, South Africa. He is named on the memorial at the cemetery.

On 8 August 1902, as a result of the award to Lieutenant Frederick Roberts, the policy in the War Office was changed and Alfred Atkinson was given the VC. In 1911 his medals were sold to Mr Spink for £70; they are now held by the Green Howards Museum, Richmond, Yorkshire.

Francis Newton PARSONS, Paardeberg, 18 February 1900

Francis Parsons was born on 23 March 1875 in Dover, Kent, the son of Doctor Charles Parsons and Venetia Digby Parsons. He was one of at least twelve children and was educated at King's College School, Cambridge and Dover College, and then at the Royal Military Academy, Sandhurst. In 1896 he enlisted into the 1st Battalion, 44th Regiment (later The Essex Regiment). He was promoted to lieutenant in March 1898 and was posted with his regiment to South Africa.

Francis Parsons.

On 18 February 1900, during the Battle of Paardeberg, Lieutenant Parsons went to the assistance of Private Ferguson, who was lying wounded on the bank of the Modder River. Parsons dressed his wounds and twice fetched water before carrying him to safety. He was under heavy fire for the whole time.

Francis Parsons was killed in action on 10 March 1900 at Driefontein and is buried in the Driefontein Cemetery – an isolated grave on the battlefield – in Orange Free State, South Africa. His VC was gazetted on 20 November 1900 and was probably posted to his family, who, in 1962, presented it to the Essex Regiment Museum, Chelmsford.

Chapter 11

Onderbank Spruit, Plewman's Farm, Hart's Hill and the Tugela Heights

Albert Edward CURTIS, Onderbank Spruit, 23 February 1900

Albert Curtis was born on 6 January 1866 in Guildford, Surrey. He began his military career with the Argyll and Sutherland Highlanders but sometime during 1893 transferred to 2nd Battalion, the East Surrey Regiment and took part in the final breakthrough by Buller at the Tugela Line, when the right flank took Monte Christo Hill.

Then, on 23 February 1900 at Onderbank Spruit (Wynne's Hill), he saw the wounded Colonel Harris lying in the open. The Boers were firing at anyone who moved and Harris was shot eight or nine times. After several efforts, Curtis succeeded in reaching him. When Curtis asked if the colonel was wounded, he replied, 'I am hit all over the body … who are you?' Curtis answered, saying, 'One of your own regiment come to try and get you away.' He attended Harris's wounds, gave him a drink and tried to carry him away but was unable to, so called for help; Private T.W. Morton came to help take him to safety. The colonel told them to leave him but they refused. Harris was found to have ten wounds.

Albert Curtis.

Curtis's grave, Bells Hill Cemetery, High Barnet, Hertfordshire.

Private Curtis was gazetted for the VC on 15 January 1901 and presented with it on 14 August that year by the Duke of Cornwall & York (later George V) at Pietermaritzburg. Private Morton was awarded the DCM. In 1910 Curtis became a Yeoman Warder at the Tower of London and held this position for twenty-one years. In 1914, Sergeant Curtis was training recruits at the East Surrey Depot, where he said to Private Harry Cator, 'Well, my boy, you must try and beat me.' He did, being awarded the VC, MM and the Croix de Guerre.

Albert Curtis died on 18 March 1940 and is buried in Bells Hill Cemetery, Plot B5, Grave 435, Spring Close, High Barnet, Hertfordshire. The grave remained unmarked until 2000. His VC is in the Ashcroft Gallery, Imperial War Museum, London.

James FIRTH, Plewman's Farm, 24 February 1900

James Firth was born on 15 January 1874 in Sheffield, Yorkshire, the son of Charles Firth, a steel smelter from Jarrow, and Elizabeth Lister, of Sheffield. He was educated at Swalwell, near Newcastle upon Tyne. Firth joined the army aged 15 in July 1889 and married Mary Edwards in 1897. He was promoted to sergeant and sailed to South Africa with the 1st Battalion, Duke of Wellington's (West Riding) Regiment.

On 24 February 1900, at Plewman's Farm near Arundel, Cape Colony, Firth carried Lance Corporal Blackman, who was wounded and exposed to enemy fire. Later

James Firth.

the same day, when the Boers had advanced to within a short distance of the firing line, he rescued Second Lieutenant T. Wilson, who was wounded and in a most exposed position, and carried him over the crest of a ridge to safety. Firth was shot through the nose and eye during this act. He lost his left eye due to his wounds and wore an eye patch for the rest of his life.

Firth's VC was gazetted (incorrectly as W. Firth) on 11 June 1901 and presented to him on 25 July that year, shortly after his return to England, by Edward VII at St James's Palace.

He left the army and found work as a foreman in a Sheffield steelworks. He had two sons: Alleyne, born 1903, and Cecil, born 1907. At the outbreak of the First World War he applied for service but was turned down due to his injury.

James Firth died from tuberculosis on 29 May 1921 and was buried in Burngreave Cemetery, Melrose Road, Sheffield, South Yorkshire. His VC passed to his oldest son but was sold in 1999 and is now in the Ashcroft Gallery, Imperial War Museum, London.

Firth's grave, Burngreave Cemetery, Sheffield, South Yorkshire.

Edgar Thomas INKSON, Hart's Hill, 24 February 1900

Edgar Inkson was born on 5 April 1872 in Nainital, India, the son of Surgeon General J. Inkson. He was educated at Edinburgh Collegiate School and received his medical education at University College Hospital, London. He joined the army as a probationary surgeon in April 1899.

Inkson was promoted to surgeon lieutenant in July 1899 and sailed to South Africa as medical officer to the 7th, 14th and 66th batteries, Royal Artillery. He was serving with these batteries at Colenso, shortly after he transferred to the 27th Inniskilling Fusiliers (Hart's Brigade). Inkson was serving with them at Spion Kop, Vaal Krantz, Pieter's Hill, and Tugela Heights.

Edgar Inkson.

On 24 February 1900, at Hart's Hill near Colenso, he carried Second Lieutenant Devenish, who was severely wounded and unable to walk,

300 or 400 yards under heavy fire, over very exposed ground, until he brought him to a place of safety.

After the relief of Ladysmith he rejoined the artillery batteries, serving with Hunter's division and then with Ian Hamilton's column. Firth went back to the Inniskilling Fusiliers in April 1901 and served with them for the remainder of the war, part of the time with Allenby's column.

In 1904 Inkson married Ethel Bromley, and they had a son and a daughter. He served throughout the First World War as a lieutenant colonel, commanding No. 2. Field Hospital, No. 1 General Hospital and

Inkson's ashes are in the family grave, Brookwood Cemetery, Woking, Surrey.

No. 4 Stationary Hospital. He was awarded the DSO in January 1917. His army service included three years at Constantinople, four years as deputy director of medical services, Gibraltar, and eleven years as medical officer to the Royal Sussex Regiment at Chichester Barracks.

Edgar Inkson died on 19 February 1947 and his ashes were interred in Brookwood Cemetery, Plot 74, Grave 211757 (family grave), Cemetery Pales, Woking, Surrey. His VC is on display at the Museum of Military Medicine, Keogh Barracks, Aldershot, Surrey.

Conwyn MANSEL-JONES, Tugela Heights, 27 February 1900

Conwyn Mansel-Jones was born on 14 June 1871 in Beddington, Surrey, youngest son of Herbert Mansel-Jones, a county court judge, and Emilia (née Davis). He was educated at Haileybury College and at the Royal Military College, Sandhurst, being commissioned into the West Yorkshire Regiment (Prince of Wales's Own) on 8 October 1890. He served with his regiment in the Ashanti Expedition of 1895–96 and in British Central Africa, 1898–99. Promoted to captain in

Conwyn Mansel-Jones.

Plewman's Farm, Hart's Hill and the Tugela Heights 111

Mansel-Jones's grave, St Nicholas's churchyard, Brockenhurst, Hampshire.

October 1899, he rejoined his regiment in Natal at the outbreak of the Boer War.

On 27 February 1900, on Terrace Hill, north of the Tugela Heights, his regiment was met with heavy shell and rifle fire and their advance was checked. Mansel-Jones rallied his men with his strong initiative and restored confidence and, although he fell severely wounded, the ridge was taken.

Despite his leg being amputated, Mansel-Jones was presented with his VC (gazetted on 27 July 1900) by the Queen at Osborne House on 20 August 1900. He was able to stay on in the army as Deputy Assistant Adjutant General for Recruiting, retiring in 1910 due to ill health. He married in 1913 and was appointed to the Bar. On the outbreak of the First World War he went to France as Deputy Assistant Adjutant General at GHQ and in 1915 was appointed Assistant Adjutant General and temporary Lieutenant Colonel. He served throughout the war, being mentioned in despatches six times, and awarded the DSO and the Legion d'Honneur.

Conwyn Mansel-Jones died on 29 May 1942 and is buried in St Nicholas's churchyard, Brockenhurst, Hampshire. His VC is not publicly held.

Chapter 12

Bloemfontein and Korn Spruit

Henry William ENGLEHEART, Bloemfontein, 13 March 1900

Henry Engleheart was born on 14 November 1863 in Blackheath, London, the son of a stockbroker and grandson of the last Queen's Proctors. He was educated at Queen Elizabeth's Grammar School in Barnet. He joined 10th Royal Hussars (Prince of Wales's Own) and sailed with them to war in South Africa.

At dawn on 13 March 1900 he was in a party of men under Major Aylmer Weston that successfully destroyed the railway line north of Bloemfontein. When returning from the raid, his party had to charge through a Boer picquet and get over four deep spruits in order to get back to their own lines. Sergeant Engleheart led the way into the first spruit, causing the enemy to flee. At the last spruit, Sapper Webb and his horse fell and were left in a dangerous position and Engleheart went back under a very heavy fire to his assistance. It took some time to get the man and his horse out of the spruit and the situation became critical as the Boers advanced on their position, but he got him out and back to their party.

Henry Engleheart.

Engleheart's VC, gazetted on 5 October 1900, was presented to him on 15 December that year by the Queen at Windsor Castle. He was one of the last five to be given the award by her. Engleheart retired from the army while in Rawalpindi, India, and became a lodge keeper at Windsor Castle.

Henry Engleheart died on 9 August 1939 following a long illness, and his ashes were scattered at Woking Crematorium, Byron Garden, Hermitage Road, St John's, Woking, Surrey. There is a memorial plaque to him at the crematorium. His VC is held by the Royal Hussars Museum, Winchester, Hampshire.

Edmund John PHIPPS-HORNBY, Korn Spruit, 31 March 1900

Edmund Phipps-Hornby was born on 31 December 1857 in Lordington, near Emsworth, Hampshire, the second son of Admiral of the Fleet Sir Geoffrey Phipps-Hornby and Emily Frances (née Coles). He was educated at a private school and at the Royal Military Academy, Woolwich, and he entered the Royal Artillery in May 1878. He took part in Sir Charles Warren's Bechuanaland Expedition of 1884–85 and was promoted to captain in 1886. Phipps-Hornby married Anna Jay in 1896 and they had two daughters. He was promoted to major the following year and was sent to South Africa on the outbreak of war in 1899.

Edmund Phipps-Hornby.

On 31 March 1900, during action at Korn Spruit, 'Q' and 'U' batteries were ambushed by the Boers, with the loss of most of the baggage and five guns of the leading battery. When the alarm was given, 'Q' Battery went into action. The Boers returned such a heavy fire that bullets were rattling on the guns like hail. As the enemy fire was too fierce for his horses to face, he ordered the guns to be retired by hand. All but one gun was saved.

Lord Roberts VC, Commander-in-Chief, South Africa, was so impressed with the gallantry displayed by all of the men in 'Q' Battery that he invoked Rule 13 of the Victoria Cross Warrant:

> It is ordained that, in the event of a gallant and daring act having been performed by a squadron, ship's company, a detached body of seamen or marines, not under fifty in number, or by a brigade, regiment, troop, or company, in which the Admiral, General, or officer commanding such forces, may deem that all are equally brave and distinguished, and that

Phipps-Hornby's grave, St Andrew's churchyard, Sonning, Berkshire.

no special selection can be made by them, then in such case the Admiral, General, or other officer commanding may direct that for any such body of seamen and marines, or for every troop or company of soldiers, one officer shall be selected by the officers engaged for the Decoration; and in like manner one petty officer or non-commissioned officer shall be selected by the petty officers and non-commissioned officers engaged; and two seamen or private soldiers or marines shall be selected by the seamen, or private soldiers, or marines engaged respectively, for the Decoration; and the names of those selected shall be transmitted by the senior officer in command of naval force, brigade, regiment, troop, or company, to the Admiral or General Officer commanding, who shall in due manner confer the Decoration as if the acts were done under his own eye.

Major Phipps-Hornby and Captain Humphreys were the only two officers present and, in the true spirit of fairness, they nominated each other, causing the authorities something of a problem! In the end the award went to Phipps-Hornby, based on his seniority. Gazetted on 26 June 1900, it was presented to him on 25 October that year by Lord Roberts VC at Pretoria.

Phipps-Hornby became ADC to Lord Roberts VC 1901–1903, when he was promoted to lieutenant colonel. He was given command of the 4th RHA Brigade at Woolwich until 1908, when he was promoted to full colonel. From 1909–13 he commanded the 4th Division as a brigadier general. On the outbreak of the First World War he commanded the III Artillery Corps, with which he was posted to France. In 1916 he took command of the artillery in the Southern Army in England until the end of the war, when he retired.

Edmund Phipps-Hornby died on 13 December 1947 and is buried in St Andrew's churchyard, High Street, Sonning, Berkshire. His VC is held by the Royal Artillery Museum (in storage), Larkhill, Wiltshire.

Charles Edward Haydon PARKER, Korn Spruit, 31 March 1900

Charles Parker was born on 10 March 1870 in St Johns, south-east London, the son of George, a veteran of the Crimean War, and Louisa Parker. He enlisted into the Royal Artillery aged 15 and served in India 1889–95, then in 1899 went to South Africa with two of his brothers, serving in the same battery.

On 31 March 1900, 'Q' and 'U' batteries were ambushed by the Boers with the loss of most of the baggage and five guns of the leading battery. When the alarm was given, 'Q' Battery went into action and Major Phipps-Hornby ordered the guns to retire. Together with Gunner Isaac Lodge and Driver Horace Glasock, Sergeant Parker helped bring the guns to safety by hand, the fire being too heavy for the horses to face. He was elected for the award by the NCOs of the regiment under Rule 13 of the Victoria Cross Warrant.

Charles Parker.

Gazetted on 26 June 1900, Parker was presented with his VC on 25 July 1901 by Edward VII at St James's Palace. After twenty-one years of service in the artillery he retired and settled in Coventry. On the outbreak of the First World War he went to work in a munitions factory, but decided to re-enlist and was posted to France. In 1918 he was invalided home, suffering from gas poisoning.

Charles Parker never recovered and died on 5 December 1918. He is buried in London Road Cemetery, Plot 198, Grave 1, London Road, Coventry, West Midlands. His VC is held by the Royal Artillery Museum (in storage), Larkhill, Wiltshire.

Parker's grave, London Road Cemetery, Coventry, West Midlands.

Horace Henry GLASOCK, Korn Spruit, 31 March 1900

Horace Glasock was born on 16 October 1880 in Islington, London. Almost nothing is known of his early life, although he joined the Royal Horse Artillery at 18 in 1898, and within a year was sailing to South Africa as part of 'Q' Battery.

He saw action at Driefontein and Bloemfontein and then, on 31 March 1900, 'Q' and 'U' batteries were ambushed by the Boers with the loss of most of the baggage and five guns of the leading battery. When the alarm was given, 'Q' Battery went into action until Major Phipps-Hornby ordered the guns to retire. Together with Sergeant Charles Parker and Gunner Isaac Lodge, Glasock helped bring the guns to safety by hand, the fire being too heavy for the horses to face. He was elected for the award by the privates of the regiment under Rule 13 of the Victoria Cross Warrant.

Horace Glasock.

Gazetted on 26 June 1900, Glasock was presented with his VC on 15 December that year by the Queen at Windsor Castle. He was one of the last five to be given the award by her. He remained in the army until 1911, when he was discharged. He then moved to Johannesburg with his wife Minnie, and they had three children. During the First World War he served as a conductor with Transports and Remounts in the South African Service Corps. He was medically discharged as unfit due to malaria, dyspepsia and liver problems.

Horace Glasock was invalided to Cape Town but died on 20 October 1916. He is buried in Maitland Road No. 4 Cemetery, Cape Town, South Africa. His VC is in the Ashcroft Gallery, Imperial War Museum, London.

Isaac LODGE, Korn Spruit, 31 March 1900

Isaac Lodge was born on 6 May 1866 in Great Canfield, Essex, the son of Elijah and Rhoda Lodge. He was educated at Great Canfield School and at 11 years old started work on a farm. He held a number of jobs before becoming a gamekeeper in charge of two woods. In December 1888 he enlisted into the Royal Garrison Artillery at Warley Barracks. He soon transferred to the Royal Horse Artillery in St John's Wood. He served in India with 'B' Battery before moving to 'Q' Battery, with which he served in India, Ireland, Newbridge Barracks and Aldershot, before they were posted to South Africa in 1899.

Isaac Lodge.

On 31 March 1900, 'Q' and 'U' batteries were ambushed by the Boers, with the loss of most of the baggage and five guns of the leading battery. When the alarm was given, 'Q' Battery went into action until Major Phipps-Hornby ordered the guns to retire. Together with Sergeant Charles Parker and Driver Horace Glasock, Lodge helped bring the guns to safety by hand, the fire being too heavy for the horses to face. He was elected for the award by the privates of the regiment under Rule 13 of the Victoria Cross Warrant.

Gazetted on 26 June 1900, he was presented with his VC on 28 October that year by Lord Roberts VC at Pretoria. After twenty-one years of service he retired from the army and returned to work as a gamekeeper, before gaining employment as a gatekeeper in the Royal Parks, first at Regent's Park, then Hyde Park.

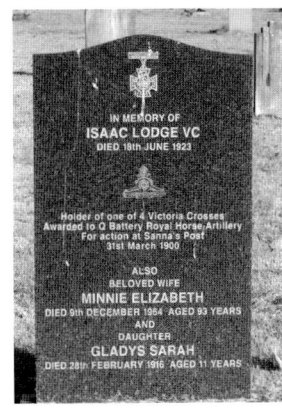

Isaac Lodge died on 18 June 1923 following an operation and is buried in Hendon Park Cemetery, Section D-9, Grave 21820, Holders Hill Road, London. His VC is held by the National Army Museum, London.

Lodge's grave, Hendon Park Cemetery, London.

Francis 'Frank' Aylmer MAXWELL, Korn Spruit, 31 March 1900

Francis Maxwell was born on 7 September 1871 in Guildford, Surrey, the son of Surgeon Major Thomas Maxwell. He joined the Royal Essex Regiment in November 1893 but transferred to the Indian Staff Corps in December, and two years later served in Waziristan and the Chitral

Expedition, where he displayed great gallantry in the recovery of the body of Lieutenant Colonel F.D. Battye, Corps of Guides, under fire, for which, although recommended, he received no award. Maxwell also served in the Tirah Expedition 1897–98, for which he was awarded the DSO.

In 1900 Maxwell volunteered to take remounts to South Africa and not long after became attached to Roberts's Light Horse.

On 31 March 1900, 'Q' and 'U' batteries were ambushed by the Boers, with the loss of most of the baggage and five guns of the leading battery. When the alarm was given, 'Q' Battery went into action under Major Phipps-Hornby, until he ordered the guns to retire. Maxwell volunteered to help the men save the guns. Fives times he went out under a hail of bullets, bringing in two guns and three limbers, one of which was dragged back by hand. He was one of those trying to bring in the last gun until the attempt had to be abandoned.

Francis Maxwell.

Maxwell was appointed ADC to Lord Kitchener, Chief-of-Staff, South Africa on 1 November 1900. Kitchener liked his outspokenness and dubbed him 'The Brat', but the two got on very well together.

Maxwell's VC was gazetted on 6 March 1900 and was presented to him on 14 August 1901 by the Duke of Cornwall & York (later George V) at Pietermaritzburg. After the war he returned to England on board the SS *Orotava* with Kitchener. In November 1902, the now Captain Maxwell was again appointed ADC to Kitchener and sailed with him to India. In 1905 he attended the Staff College at Camberley, and in 1906 married Charlotte Alice Hamilton and they had two daughters. In 1910–16, Major Maxwell was Military Secretary to Lord Hardinge, Governor General of India. During the First World War he commanded the 12th Battalion of the Middlesex Regiment and was awarded a Bar to his DSO.

Maxwell's grave, Ypres Reservoir Cemetery, North Ypres, Belgium.

Brigadier General Francis Maxwell was commanding the 27th Infantry Brigade, 9th Scottish Division when shot and killed by a sniper near Ypres on 21 September 1917. One of the most senior officers to be killed in action, he is buried in Ypres Reservoir Cemetery, Plot I, Row A, Grave 37, North Ypres, Belgium. His VC is in the Ashcroft Gallery, Imperial War Museum, London.

Chapter 13

Wakkerstroom, Crow's Nest Hill, Delagoa Bay Railway, Lindley, Wolve Spruit and Krugersdorp

William Henry Snyder NICKERSON, Wakkerstroom, 20 April 1900

William Nickerson was born on 27 March 1875 in Dorchester, New Brunswick, Canada, the son of the Reverend D. Nickerson, Chaplain to the Armed Forces. He was educated at Portsmouth Grammar School and Owen's College (forerunner of the University of Manchester), graduating in medicine in 1896 and joining the RAMC in 1898. Within a year he was posted to South Africa.

William Nickerson.

On 20 April 1900, while attached to the Mounted Infantry, he went out under rifle and shellfire and stitched up the stomach of a man whose entrails were protruding. He then stayed with him until the fire slackened and the stretcher-bearers arrived. For his service he was promoted to captain in November 1900. His VC, gazetted on 12 February 1901, was presented to him on 14 August 1901 by the Duke of Cornwall & York (later George V) in Pietermaritzburg.

Promoted to major in 1909, Nickerson served with the cavalry in the 1914 retreat, 1st and 2nd Ypres, Neuve Chapelle, on the Somme in 1915 and, from December 1915, at Salonika, Greece. He was promoted to lieutenant colonel in 1916.

In 1918 he married Nan Waller and they had a son and a daughter. Nickerson was Honorary Surgeon to the King 1925–33 and Colonel Commandant of the RAMC until 1945. During this time he served on an Atlantic convoy, and with the Port of London Emergency Service and the Home Guard.

William Nickerson died on 10 April 1954 and is buried in a private burial ground at his home in Cour, Kintyre, Scotland. His VC is not publicly held.

Harry Churchill BEET, Wakkerstroom, 22 April 1900

Harry Beet.

Harry Beet was born on 1 April 1873 at Brackendale Farm, near Bingham, Nottinghamshire, the son of J.A. Beet, a sculptor. He joined the Derbyshire Regiment (Sherwood Foresters) in February 1892 and two years later sailed for India, seeing service in the Tirah Expedition 1897–98 on the North-West Frontier, following which he was posted to South Africa.

On 22 April 1900, during the retreat from a farm under a ridge held by the Boers, Corporal Burnett was left on the ground wounded. On seeing him, Corporal Beet remained behind, placed him under cover and dressed his wounds. He also kept up such a heavy fire that the Boers were prevented from approaching until dark. He was under very heavy fire the whole time.

Beet's VC, gazetted on 12 February 1901, was presented to him on 14 August that year by the Duke of Cornwall & York (later George V) in Pietermaritzburg. He was promoted to sergeant by Lord Kitchener for his services. Beet was later wounded near Virginia on 9 December 1901. He was then promoted to captain and soon after the end of the war he emigrated to Saskatchewan, Canada.

On the outbreak of the First World War, Beet enlisted into the 32nd Reserve Canadian Infantry Battalion and served in France with the Canadian Expeditionary Force (CEF). Very little is known about the rest of his life. He died on 10 January 1946 and is buried in Mountain View Cemetery, Veteran's Section, Abray Section, Block 3, Plot 5, Lot 12, Prince Edward Avenue, Vancouver, British Columbia, Canada. His VC is held by the Sherwood Foresters Museum, The Castle, Nottingham.

John Frederick MACKAY, Crow's Nest Hill, 20 May 1900

John MacKay was born on 6 June 1873 in Edinburgh. After a private education he attended the University of Edinburgh, before enlisting in the Gordon Highlanders. He served with the 1st Battalion on the North-West Frontier and in the Tirah Expedition 1897–98. On the outbreak of the Boer War he was posted to South Africa with his battalion.

He saw action at Magersfontein and Paardeberg. On 20 May 1900, at Crows Nest Hill, near Johannesburg, MacKay repeatedly went forward under heavy fire to attend to wounded comrades, far from any cover. He carried one man from open ground to shelter under heavy fire.

John MacKay.

MacKay saw more action at Pretoria, Belfast and the Eastern Transvaal. On 11 July 1900, he fought at Wolvekrantz, near Krugersdorp, and was again recommended for the VC (it would not be possible for him to be awarded a second or Bar to his VC for this action as the rules state you must already be in possession of the VC to be eligible for a second award). His VC (for the 20 May action) was gazetted on 10 August 1900 and was presented to him on 25 October that year by Lord Roberts VC at Pretoria.

In 1903, MacKay served with the Southern Nigeria Regiment, accompanying the expedition to the Ime River, Cross River and Ibibio Country in 1904–1905, and the Bende Hinterland Expedition in 1905–1906. In 1907 he transferred to the Argyll and Sutherland Highlanders in command of the Ogumi Patrol. He served in France during the First World War in 1915–16. On returning home he was given command of 2nd/6th Battalion, Highland Light Infantry, a post he held until the unit was disbanded. His last promotion to lieutenant colonel saw him in command of the 1st Battalion, Argyll and Sutherland Highlanders, in India in 1919.

After his retirement John MacKay moved to the south of France, where he died on 9 January 1930 and is buried in Cimetiere de Caucade, Plot 42, Nice. His VC is held by the Gordon Highlanders Museum, Aberdeen.

Frank Howard KIRBY, Delagoa Bay Railway, 2 June 1900

Frank Kirby was born on 12 November 1871 in Thame, Oxfordshire, the son of William and Ade Kirby. He was educated at the fee-paying Alleyn's School, Dulwich, London. He entered the Royal Engineers at St George's Barracks, London, in August 1892 and was posted to South Africa with the Field Troops, Royal Engineers in 1899.

Frank Kirby.

Kirby was awarded the DCM for blowing up the Bloemfontein Railway in March 1900. On 2 June 1900 he was in a party sent to cut the Delagoa Bay Railway. While retreating they were attacked by a large number of Boers. One man had his horse shot from under him. Corporal Kirby went back towards the enemy under heavy fire, picked him up and rode back to rejoin his troop. His action undoubtedly saved the man's life.

Kirby was promoted to troop sergeant major in the field by Lord Roberts VC in July 1900. He was mentioned in despatches and his VC was gazetted on 8 October 1900. He was presented with it on 19 August 1901 by the Duke of Cornwall & York (later George V) in Cape Town.

Kirby was made a warrant officer in 1906 and in 1909 married Kate Jolly, with whom he had two sons and two daughters. In April 1911, he was commissioned a lieutenant from the ranks and the following year was gazetted into the Royal Flying Corps, in which he became a squadron commander. He served in France during the First World War and was a temporary lieutenant colonel by the end of the conflict.

Frank Kirby died on 8 July 1956 and his ashes are interred at South London Crematorium, (aka Streatham Vale Crematorium), Section Q-29, The Loggia Garden, Rowan Road, Streatham Vale. His VC is in the Ashcroft Gallery, Imperial War Museum, London.

Charles Burley WARD, Lindley, 26 June 1900

Charles Ward.

Charles Ward was born on 10 July 1877 in Hunslet, near Leeds, West Yorkshire, the son of George Ward. He was educated at Primrose Hill School in Leeds and in April 1897 enlisted into the 1st Battalion, Yorkshire Light Infantry (the old 54th Regiment of Foot). He served with this battalion for two years and transferred to the 2nd Battalion while in South Africa at the outset of the Boer War.

On 26 June 1900, a picquet of his regiment was attacked by 500 Boers from three sides. Reinforcements were needed and Private Ward volunteered to deliver the message. His offer was at first refused but he insisted. Crossing 150 yards of open ground under fire, he delivered the message and returned from a place of safety to inform his commander that reinforcements were on the way. Ward was severely wounded during his return trip but his action undoubtedly saved the outpost.

Ward's wounds were so bad he was invalided home and forced to leave the army. His VC, gazetted on 28 September 1900, was presented to him on 15 December that year by the Queen at Windsor Castle. He was one of the last five to be given the award by her.

During the First World War, Ward was an instructor, but his life took a turn for the worse as he was deeply troubled by his experiences in South Africa and was admitted to the Glamorgan County Asylum in Bridgend, where he died on 30 December 1921. Charles Ward is buried in St Mary's churchyard, Section B, Row 2, Grave 8/4, Bute Street, Whitchurch, Cardiff. His VC is not publicly held.

A silent film interview with Private Ward following his award of the VC was made by Lancashire cinematographers Sager Mitchell and James Kenyon. The film roll was sealed in a steel barrel after their company went out of business in the 1920s. It was rediscovered during demolition work in 1994 and has been restored by the British Film Institute.

Arthur Herbert Lindsay RICHARDSON, Wolve Spruit, 5 July 1900

Arthur Richardson was born on 23 September 1872 in Southport, near Liverpool. Nothing is known of his early life until he emigrated to Canada in 1891 or 1892, where he worked as a dentist before joining the North-West Mounted Police in May 1894 and was promoted to corporal in 1898. At the outbreak of the Boer War he was given leave from the Mounted Police to enlist into the Lord Strathcona's Horse, a Canadian unit.

On 5 July 1900, at Wolve Spruit, 15 miles north of Standerton, he was in a party of thirty-eight men who became engaged with eighty Boers. When the order was given to retire, Sergeant Richardson spotted a badly wounded comrade who had been thrown from his horse. He rode back towards the Boers, picked the man up and carried him to safety. He was under heavy fire the whole time and his own horse was wounded.

Arthur Richardson.

Richardson travelled briefly to England to be presented with his VC (gazetted on 14 September 1900) by Edward VII at St James's Palace on 25 July 1901, before returning to South Africa, where he saw more action. After the war he returned to Canada and as a token of their esteem, his fellow Canadians presented him with £3,000. Richardson returned to work with the Mounted Police, becoming a sergeant major, but due to poor health he purchased his release in 1907. He took up work as the town constable of Indian Head, Saskatchewan, but became debt-ridden and pawned his medals. He returned to England in 1909 and became something of a recluse, living in poverty. During this time another man named Arthur Richardson, a

Richardson's gravestone, St James's Cemetery (now a park), St James Road, Liverpool.

corporal in the Gordon Highlanders, began passing himself off as the recipient of the VC. So successful was he that, on his death, he was buried with military honours. Ironically, Richardson, the real VC holder, was discovered marching in the funeral cortège of his imposter! As a result he rose to a certain prominence in his middle age.

Arthur Richardson died from appendicitis on 15 December 1932 and is buried in St James's Cemetery (now a park), Plot 57679 (headstone reads 'buried within this cemetery'), St James Road, Liverpool. His VC is held by the National Archives of Canada, Ottawa, Ontario.

William Eagleson GORDON, Krugersdorp, 11 July 1900

William Gordon was born on 4 May 1866 at Bridge of Allan, near Stirling, Scotland, the son of W.E. Gordon MD. He joined the militia in 1886 as lieutenant in the Royal Artillery and then joined the Gordon Highlanders in June 1888. He served in the Chitral Relief Expedition of 1895 and then on the North-West Frontier during the Tirah Expedition of 1897–98 as a captain.

He served as adjutant of the 1st Battalion from January 1900 and throughout the Boer War. Gordon was badly wounded at Magersfontein and was attended to on the battlefield by Lieutenant Douglas, who was awarded the VC for doing so (see Chapter 3). He also saw action at Paardeberg, Poplar Grove, Driefontein, Hontnek, Vet River and Hand River.

William Gordon.

On 11 July 1900, Captain Gordon, with Captian Younger, took out a party of men who successfully dragged an artillery wagon under cover of a small kopje, while exposed to very heavy and accurate fire. Then Gordon went out alone to fasten the drag rope to the gun. Having done this he called for volunteers to pull in the gun. While moving the gun four men were wounded, Younger mortally so. Gordon ordered the men to take cover and, again alone, attended to the wounded. Gordon saw more action at Doornkop, Belfast and Lydenburg.

He was presented with his VC (gazetted on 28 September 1900) by Lord Kitchener at Pretoria on 8 June 1902, and sailed home with his battalion in September, when he married and had one son. Gordon was appointed Staff Captain, Gordon Highland Grouped Regimental District 1903–1908 and was promoted to major in January 1907. In 1908–1909 he was Deputy Assistant Adjutant and Quartermaster General to the Highland Division, Scottish Command. In 1913 he was appointed ADC to George V, with the brevet of colonel.

Gordon's grave, St Alban's churchyard, Hindhead, Surrey.

He served in France during the First World War until taken prisoner. He was released by exchange in 1916 and took command of No. 1 Midland District, Scottish Command. He won £500 damages when the *People's Journal* falsely claimed he had ordered the Gordons to surrender during the retreat from Mons in 1914.

William Gordon and his wife were injured in an air raid in November 1940 and he died as a result of his wounds on 10 March 1941. He is buried in St Alban's churchyard, East Block, Grave 76, Tilford Road, Hindhead, Surrey. His VC is held by the Gordon Highlanders Museum, Aberdeen.

David Reginald YOUNGER, Krugersdorp, 11 July 1900

David Younger was born on 17 March 1871 in Edinburgh and was educated at St Ninian's School, Moffat and Malvern College 1885–90. He was commissioned into the Duke of Edinburgh's Edinburgh Artillery in 1891 and transferred to the Gorgon Highlanders in 1893. Younger took part in the Chitral Expedition of 1895 and then on the North-West Frontier during the Tirah Expedition of 1897–1898.

David Younger.

On 11 July 1900 he, with Captain Gordon, took out a party of men who successfully dragged an artillery wagon under cover of a small kopje, while exposed to very heavy and accurate fire. Then Gordon went out alone to fasten the drag rope to the gun. Having done this he called for volunteers to pull in the gun. He accompanied the party of volunteers but while moving the gun four men were wounded, Younger dying shortly after. He is buried in Krugersdorp Cemetery, Halgryn Street, Krugersdorp, South Africa. His VC (gazetted on 28 September 1900 & 8 August 1902) was sent to his family by registered post and is not publicly held.

Neville Reginald HOWSE, Vredefort, 24 July 1900

Neville Howse was born on 26 October 1863 in Stogursey, Somerset, the son of Alfred Howse, a surgeon, and Lucy Elizabeth (née Conroy). He was educated at Fullard's House School, Taunton, and studied medicine at the London Hospital, qualifying in April 1884, and becoming a member of the Royal College of Surgeons in 1886. The following year he became a licentiate of the Royal College of Practitioners.

Howse emigrated to Australia in 1889 and worked as a country doctor at the Manning River Hospital in New South Wales, but he returned to England in 1896 for professional development. He qualified as a surgeon the following year and returned to Australia, where he was commissioned into the NSW Army Medical Corps. He was promoted to lieutenant and sent to serve in South Africa.

Neville Howse.

Howse attended the wounded Gordon Highlanders after their action at Doornkop on 20 May 1900, working through the night in bell tents with candles for lighting.

On 24 July 1900, the NSW Mounted Rifles attacked General de Wet's rearguard near Vredefort. Shot though the bladder, a young trumpeter lay wounded. Howse rode through very heavy crossfire to reach the man.

However, his horse was soon shot from under him, so he grabbed his medical bag and continued on foot until he reached him and dressed his wound. He then picked him up and carried him over his shoulder to safety. Years later he dismissed his VC action as 'nothing more than a fit of insanity'.

Howse returned to Australia in January 1901 and was presented with his VC (gazetted on 4 June 1900) by the Chief Justice of NSW, Sir Frederick Darley. This was the first VC awarded to an Australian unit and the only one to a medical officer. In February 1902 Howse returned to South Africa in command of the 1st Australian Commonwealth Bearer Company, with the rank of major.

In 1905 he married Evelyn Pilcher and they had two sons and three daughters. When the First World War broke out he immediately volunteered for active service. On 14 August 1914, Howse was appointed to the Australian Naval and Military Expeditionary Force as Principal Medical Officer with the rank of lieutenant colonel.

In Gallipoli he found very poor medical practices being carried out. Lightly wounded men were being sent to hospital ships with beds

Howse's grave, Kensal Green Cemetery, London.

while more seriously wounded men were placed on ships with skeleton crews. The beaches were jammed with wounded and eventually Howse managed to evacuate some 1,200 men in two days. He was also involved in the truce held on 24 May 1915 to help bury the dead from no man's land. Howse suffered from dysentery and had to be evacuated to Egypt for a short time. After the attack at Lone Pine he worked twleve hours straight, dealing with 700 wounded, and the next day he was slightly wounded himself.

While in England in 1919, Howse was heavily involved with the repatriation of the sick and wounded. He also arranged for his doctors and nurses to take up free postgraduate study in British universities and hospitals. He returned to Australia in January 1920. In 1922 he resigned his commission in the army to enter politics, as regulations at the time forbade political campaigning by members of the armed forces. He served in politics until 1929, when he lost his seat in the Labour landslide. Howse decided to go back to medical practice, returning to England to refresh his surgical skills. While there he was diagnosed with gallstones. An operation revealed pancreatic cancer.

Neville Howse died on 19 September 1930 and is buried in Kensal Green Cemetery, Square 14, Row 4, Grave 49245, Harrow Road, London. His VC is on display at the Australian War Memorial, Canberra. In 2000, a postage stamp commemorating Howse's VC action was issued by Australia Post.

Chapter 14

Vredefort, Mosilikatse Nek, Essenbosch Farm, Van Wyk's Vlei, Geluk and Bergendal

William John HOUSE, Mosilikatse Nek, 2 August 1900

William House was born on 7 October 1879 in Thatcham, near Newbury, Berkshire, the son of Thomas House (a labourer) and Sally (née Owen). He joined the Royal Berkshire Regiment (Princess Charlotte of Wales's) in November 1896 and within three years was sailing to South Africa on the outbreak of the Boer War.

During the attack on Mosilikatse Nek, on 2 August 1900, when Sergeant Gibbs, who had gone forward to reconnoitre, was wounded, Private House rushed out from cover (although cautioned not to do so, as the fire from the enemy was very hot), picked up the wounded man and endeavoured to bring him to safety. In doing so, House was wounded in the neck and head, and although in great pain, he called out to his comrades not to risk their lives coming to his aid.

House's VC, gazetted on 7 October 1902 (his twenty-third birthday), was presented to him on 24 October that year by Edward VII in London. After recovering from his wounds he remained in the army and saw service in India, before returning to England in November 1911. However, his life was

William House.

House's grave, St James Cemetery, Dover, Kent.

tragically cut short. While at Dover's Shafts Barracks, on 28 February 1912 he was cleaning his rifle and it discharged, killing him. The *Dover Express* reported that he had committed suicide 'owing to his brain being unhinged either by the wound he had received at the time he gained the VC, or from his subsequent service in India'.

William House is buried in St James Cemetery, Section N, Grave 1–16, Old Charlton Road, Dover, Kent. His VC is held by the Royal Gloucestershire, Berkshire & Wiltshire Regiment Museum, Salisbury, Wiltshire.

Brian Turner Tom LAWRENCE, Essenbosch Farm, 7 August 1900

Brian Lawrence.

Brain Lawrence was born on 9 November 1873 in Bewdley, Worcestershire, one of five sons to John and Hannah Lawrence. He was educated at the King Charles I Grammar School, Kidderminster. Lawrence was an excellent horseman and joined the 17th Lancers (Duke of Cambridge's Own) and, by the start of the Boer War, was a sergeant.

On 7 August 1900, near Essenbosch Farm, while on patrol with Private Hayman they were attacked by twelve or fourteen Boers. Hayman's horse was shot and he was thrown from it, dislocating his shoulder. Lawrence dismounted, lifted Hayman onto his own horse and told him to ride back to their piquet line. He then walked for 2 miles, keeping the enemy at bay with their two carbines until help arrived.

Lawrence was presented with his VC, gazetted on 15 January 1901, by Edward VII in London on 12 August 1902. He then became a riding master in the 18th Hussars and was promoted to honorary lieutenant. Lawrence was a member of the 1912 Olympic team, along with Paul Kenna VC.

Lawrence fought in the First World War and was seriously wounded in 1914. He was promoted to captain in December 1915, major in 1917 and lieutenant colonel in 1923. In 1923–26 he served on the General Staff,

Iraq Levies, and in 1925–26 commanded a mobile force in Kurdistan. Lawrence married Nancy Leijel, from Mansfield. In 1934–38 he was a Military Knight of Windsor. He served in the Second World War at Whitehall until 1942.

Brian Lawrence emigrated to Kenya and died there on 7 June 1949. He was cremated at Nakuru Crematorium, Kenya. His VC is in the Ashcroft Gallery, Imperial War Museum, London.

Harry HAMPTON, Van Wyk's Vlei, 21 August 1900

Harry Hampton was born on 14 December 1870 in Richmond, Surrey, the son of Samuel Hampton. He enlisted into the 1st Battalion, the King's (Liverpool) Regiment, at Aldershot in March 1889 and was promoted to corporal in 1891. He served in the West Indies and Nova Scotia in 1891–97.

In South Africa he was present at the siege of Ladysmith and supported the defenders of Wagon Hill. After the siege he took part in the advance into the Transvaal with the 1st Mounted Infantry Company (attached to his regiment). On 21 August 1900, at Van Wyk's

Harry Hampton.

Vlei, Sergeant Hampton was in command of a small party of mounted infantry. He held an important position for some time against heavy odds and, when forced to retire, saw all of his men safely into cover. Then, although he had been wounded in the head, he helped Lance Corporal Walsh, who was unable to walk, until the man was hit again and killed, Hampton being wounded again shortly after.

His VC, gazetted on 18 October 1901, was presented to him on 17 December that year by Edward VII at St James's Palace. After the war he was promoted to colour sergeant and appointed Sergeant Instructor of Musketry, before being discharged on a pension. He married and had two children. Hampton returned to the Richmond area and took up work as a grocery manager. Due to his injuries from the Boer War he was not considered fit for service in the First World War.

Harry Hampton died on 2 November 1922 after sustaining multiple injuries when he fell against a passing steam train at Richmond. The inquest determined that, due to an old injury, his leg gave way and he stumbled into the train. He is buried in Richmond Cemetery, Old Church Ground, Section X, Grave 62, Lower Grove Road, Richmond upon Thames, Surrey. His grave was unmarked and was thought lost, but in 1986 Ron Buddle, a police officer, discovered the grave site and with help from the King's Regiment a headstone was placed on his grave. His VC is held by the King's (Liverpool) Regiment Museum, Liverpool.

Hampton's grave, Richmond Cemetery, Richmond upon Thames, Surrey.

Henry James KNIGHT, Van Wyk's Vlei, 21 August 1900

Henry Knight was born (James Huntley Knight) on 5 November 1878 in Yeovil, Somerset. Little is known about his early life, but it seems he enlisted (under the name Henry James Knight) into the 1st Battalion, the King's (Liverpool) Regiment, after the death of his father; the reason for the name change is unknown.

On 21 August 1900, during operations at Van Wyk's Vlei, Corporal Knight was posted in some rocks with four men, covering the rear of a detachment of the company, when they were attacked by fifty Boers. He ordered his small party to retire one by one to better cover while he maintained his position for nearly an hour. He lost two men and, when he retired, he carried a wounded man for 2 miles, under fire the whole time.

Henry Knight.

His VC, gazetted on 4 January 1901, was presented to him On 8 June 1902 by Lord Kitchener at Pretoria, and he was promoted to sergeant.

Knight joined the Manchester Regiment as a temporary lieutenant in February 1915 and by March was promoted to captain. He testified in a scandal centred on illegal payments involving his regiment and then in October 1915 resigned his commission. The following month he enlisted into the London (Scottish) Regiment. Promoted to corporal, he was sent to France and was wounded at Gommecourt in July 1916.

Henry Knight died on 24 November 1955 and his ashes were scattered at Bournemouth Crematorium, Garden of Remembrance, Strouden Avenue, Bournemouth, Dorset. He is named (as James Huntley Knight) on his wife's headstone at the churchyard of Milborne St Andrew, Dorset. Knight's VC is held by the King's (Liverpool) Regiment Museum, Liverpool.

Knight is named (as James Huntley Knight) on his wife's headstone at the churchyard of Milborne St Andrew, Dorset.

William Edward HEATON, Geluk, 23 August 1900

William Heaton was born on 2 January 1875 in Ormskirk, Lancashire, the oldest of three children born to Robert and Alice Heaton. At 24 he enlisted into the 1st Battalion, the King's (Liverpool) Regiment, and within a year was sailing for service in South Africa.

On 23 August 1900, his company were advancing ahead of the general line and became surrounded by Boers. As they started to suffer severely, at the request of his commanding officer Heaton volunteered to take a message back asking for relief. Under heavy fire, he accomplished his mission at imminent risk to his life. Had he not done so, the company would have had to surrender or be wiped out.

William Heaton.

Heaton's VC, gazetted on 18 January 1901, was presented to him on 14 August that year by the Duke of Cornwall & York (later George V) at Pietermaritzburg. Later he served with the 6th (Rifle) Battalion, King's Regiment and saw action in northern France and Flanders. After the war he returned to Ormskirk.

Heaton's grave, Ormskirk Parish churchyard, Southport, Lancashire.

William Heaton died on 5 June 1941 and is buried in Ormskirk Parish churchyard, Plot 111, Church Street, Southport, Lancashire. His VC is held by the King's (Liverpool) Regiment Museum, Liverpool.

Alfred Edward DURRANT, Bergendal, 27 August 1900

Alfred Durrant was born on 4 November 1864 in Westminster, London. Little is known about his early life before he enlisted into the 2nd Battalion, Rifle Brigade (Prince Consort's Own) just prior to the outbreak of the Boer War.

On 27 August 1900, at the Battle of Bergendal, Acting Corporal Wellar, having been wounded and somewhat dazed, got up from his prone position in the firing line, exposing himself even more to the enemy's fire, and commenced to run towards them. Private Durrant rose from his prone position, caught up with Wellar and pulled him down, endeavouring to keep him calm but, finding this impossible, he picked him up and carried him for 200 yards under a heavy fire back to a place of safety. Then he returned to his place in the firing line.

Alfred Durrant.

Durrant's VC, gazetted on 18 October 1901, was presented to him on 6 October 1902 by Lord Kitchener and he was promoted to lance corporal for his service in South Africa. He was later awarded the Imperial Service Medal for 25 years' service. Almost nothing is known about his later life.

Alfred Durrant died on 29 March 1933 and is buried in Tottenham Cemetery, Rosery Section, Grave 221, White Hart Lane, London. His VC is held by the Royal Green Jackets Museum, Winchester, Hampshire.

Durrant's grave, Tottenham Cemetery, London.

Chapter 15

Warm Baths, Geluk, Zeerust, Komati River, Dewetsdorp and Nooitgedacht Hill

John Hutton BISDEE, Warm Baths, 1 September 1900

John Bisdee was born on 28 September 1869 in Hutton Park, Melton Mowbray, Tasmania. He was educated at Hutchins School in Hobart before working on his father's property until he enlisted into the 1st Tasmanian Imperial Bushmen for service in South Africa.

On 1 September 1900, Trooper Bisdee was one of the advance scouting party passing through a narrow gorge at Warm Baths (Warm Bad) under the command of Lieutenant Guy Wylly, when the Boers opened fire at close range and six out of eight men were hit,

John Bisdee.

including two officers, Major Brooke and Lieutenant Wylly. Brooke's horse had bolted so Bisdee dismounted and placed him on his horse, mounted behind him and rode him out of range of the enemy. Bisdee was wounded during this action and was invalided home.

His VC, gazetted on 13 November 1900, was presented to him on 11 August 1902 by the Governor of Tasmania in Hobart. Bisdee returned to farming and in April 1904 married Georgina Hale. Two years later he joined the 12th Australian Light Horse and by 1910 was a captain. During the First World War he saw service in the Egyptian Senussi Campaign, until a leg wound precluded further action service. He continued to serve and in 1918 was appointed Assistant Provost Marshall of the ANZAC Day Provost Corps. After the war, he again returned to farming.

John Bisdee died from chronic nephritis on 14 January 1930 and is buried in St James churchyard, Tranquillity, Tasmania. His VC is held by the Tasmanian Museum & Art Gallery, Hobart.

Guy George Egerton WYLLY, Warm Baths, 1 September 1900

Guy Wylly.

Guy Wylly was born on 17 February 1880 in Hobart, Tasmania, the son of Edward Arthur Egerton Wylly, formerly of the 109th Regiment and Madras Staff Corps. As an infant Guy accompanied his parents to India before returning to Hobart in 1885. He attended the Hutchins School, Hobart, and completed his education at the Collegiate School of St Peter, Adelaide.

In April 1900, Wylly embarked for South Africa as a lieutenant with the 3rd (1st Tasmanian Imperial). After its arrival in South Africa the unit was absorbed into the 4th Imperial Bushmen, which, by August, was constantly under enemy fire in small engagements. On 1 September 1900, Wylly was commanding an advance scouting party passing through a narrow gorge at Warm Baths (Warm Bad) when the Boers opened fire at close range and six out of eight men were hit, including Wylly. Seeing that one of his men (Corporal E.S. Brown) was badly wounded and his horse was shot from under him, Wylly went back to help him. He made the wounded man take his horse while he opened fire from behind a rock on the advancing Boers to cover the retreat of the others, at the imminent risk of himself being cut off. Brown's brother, who was also wounded in the ambush, died later from his wounds.

Wylly's VC was gazetted on 23 November 1900 and presented to him on 25 July 1901 by Edward VII at St James's Palace. Transferring to the British Army, Wylly served first with the Berkshires, and then the Lancashire Regiment, with whom he served in India. In 1902 he transferred into the Indian Army, serving with the 46th Punjab Regiment in 1902–1904. In 1909 he was appointed ADC to the Commander-in-Chief, India, Lord Kitchener.

Having qualified at the Staff College in India, Wylly was posted as a captian to the Mhow Cavalry Brigade, serving with the BEF in France, and was wounded in 1915. After his recovery he was briefly posted to the staff in the 4th British Division in 1916, before taking a position in the

3rd Australian Division. From February 1916 to July 1917, he was on the staff of the 1st ANZAC Corps, his final appointment before returning to India in 1919–30, and was ADC to the King from 1926 to 1933. For his service in the First World War he was mentioned in despatches three times.

Guy Wylly died on 9 January 1962 and his ashes were scattered at Woking Crematorium, Tennyson Lake Garden, Garden of Remembrance, Hermitage Road, St John's, Woking, Surrey. His VC is held by the Tasmanian Museum & Art Gallery, Hobart.

Edward Douglas BROWN (later BROWN-SYNGE-HUTCHINSON), Geluk, 13 October 1900

Edward Douglas Brown was born on 6 March 1861 in Dagshai, India, the son of Major David Philip Brown (7th Queen's Own Hussars) and Frances (née Synge-Hutchinson). He was educated at Edinburgh Academy, Windermere College, and the United Services College, Westward Ho! Brown was commissioned a lieutenant in the 18th Hussars in November 1883 and was a captain within five years. In March 1889 he exchanged into the 14th Hussars and, from January 1890 to December 1894, was commandant of the Aldershot School of Instruction for Yeomanry. Brown was promoted to major just prior to his service in the Boer War.

Edward Brown.

In South Africa he was mentioned in despatches for the retirement at Thaba 'Nchu, and for leading the most advanced position during the Battle of Diamond Hill. Then, on 13 October 1900 at Geluk, when the enemy were within 400 yards and bringing a heavy fire to bear, Major Brown, seeing Sergeant Hersey's horse was shot, stopped and helped him onto his own horse and rode him to safety. Shortly afterwards he held Lieutenant Brown's horse steady so he could mount, and finally he carried Lance Corporal Leigh, who was wounded, out of the action. All of these acts were carried out under heavy fire.

Brown's VC, gazetted on 15 January 1901, was presented to him on 14 August that year by the Duke of Cornwall & York (later George V) at Pietermaritzburg. He was then promoted to lieutenant colonel and commanded the 14th Hussars for the remainder of the war.

In 1904 he changed his name to Brown-Synge-Hutchinson. In 1906 he was promoted to brevet colonel, and in 1911 was made Knight of Grace of the Order of St John of Jerusalem, in England. He was also appointed a member of the Executive Committee of the St John Ambulance Association, a post he held until 1919. Brown-Synge-Hutchinson was also awarded the Freedom of the City of London in 1911. In March 1917, he was promoted to Knight of Justice of St John of Jerusalem. It is believed he grew a large moustache to hide a sword cut.

Edward Brown-Synge-Hutchinson died on 3 March 1940 and his ashes were scattered at Golders Green Crematorium, Disposal Lawns, Hoop Lane, London. His VC is held by the 14th/20th (King's) Hussars Museum, Preston, Lancashire.

Colonel Edward Brown-Synge-Hutchinson is one of the VC recipients remembered on a plaque at Golders Green Crematorium, London, where his ashes are scattered.

Alexis Charles DOXAT, Zeerust, 20 October 1900

Alexis Doxat was born on 9 April 1867 in Surbiton, Surrey, the son of Edmund Doxat of Wood Park Green, Hertfordshire. He was educated at Norwich Grammar School and Philberd's, Maidenhead. He became a captain in the Dalston Militia and passed the Auxiliary School of Instruction and the Hythe Musketry School. He was a member of the Stock Exchange but resigned this position on the outbreak of the Boer War.

Alexis Doxat.

From May 1900, Doxat took part in Lord Methuen's advance from Boshof and, in September, joined General Douglas's column as personal ADC, acting as a reconnaissance officer. On 20 October 1900, near Zeerust, Lieutenant Doxat proceeded with a party of mounted infantry to reconnoitre a position held by 100 Boers on a ridge of kopjes. Within 300 yards, his men came under heavy fire. As his party retired Doxat saw one man thrown from his wounded horse and left in a dangerous position. Doxat galloped back, took the man on his own horse and rode him to a place of safety.

Doxat's grave, City Cemetery (aka Newmarket Road Cemetery), Cambridge.

Doxat's VC, gazetted on 15 January 1901, was presented to him on 17 December that year by Edward VII at Marlborough House, London. He married Emma Collison Mair in 1903. He served in the First World War, being awarded the 1914–15 Star, the War Medal and the Victory Medal (Pip, Squeak and Wilfred). He was invalided out of the army in 1918.

Alexis Doxat died on 29 November 1942 and is buried in City Cemetery (aka Newmarket Road Cemetery), Section 15, Grave 8154, Newmarket Road, Cambridge. His VC is in the Ashcroft Gallery, Imperial War Museum, London.

Hampden Zane Churchill COCKBURN, Komati River, 7 November 1900

Hampden Cockburn was born on 19 November 1867 in Toronto, Ontario, Canada, the son of George Ralph Richardson Cockburn, a director of the Ontario Bank and MP for the city of Toronto and Principal of Upper Canada College. Hampden was educated at Upper Canada College, and later at Rugby School, England. In November 1891 he entered the Governor General's Bodyguard, with the rank of second lieutenant. He was awarded the Royal Canadian Humane Society's Medal for saving the lives of two brothers, Robert and James Harris, who were drowning in Lake Rousseau on 20 September 1897.

In early 1900 he volunteered for service in the Boer War with the Royal Canadian Dragoons. At Leliefontein, Komati River, near Belfast, in Mpumalanga Province, on 7 November 1900, General Smith-Dorrien had forced the Boers out of a strong position, which they attempted to recover after they had been reinforced but were prevented from doing so by the 84th Battery. On the return march the Royal Canadian Dragoons acted as a rearguard,

Hampden Cockburn.

holding back 200 mounted Boers. Lieutenant Cockburn and Lieutenant Turner, with Sergeant Holland, tried to stop them from capturing two 12-pounder guns. Cockburn and a few men held them off long enough to enable the guns to be got safely away, Cockburn being wounded at this time. When the Boers again threatened to capture the guns, Holland used his Colt revolver to deadly effect, until finding the enemy almost on top of him. Turner, although twice wounded, then dismounted and deployed some men at close quarters and drove off the Boers. All of the men under his command were killed, wounded or captured during this action. By the war's end, Cockburn had taken part in forty-five engagements.

Cockburn's VC, gazetted on 23 April 1901, was presented to him on 11 October that year by the Duke of Cornwall & York (later George V) in Toronto. Following his return to Canada, Cockburn was promoted to major and belonged to the Canadian Reserve of Officers.

Hampden Cockburn retired to run a ranch but was tragically killed as a result of a riding accident on 12 July 1913. He is buried in St James Cemetery, Hill A, Section S 1/2, Lot 11, Toronto, Ontario. His VC was donated to his old school, the Upper Canada College, and is currently on loan to the Canadian War Museum, Ottawa, Ontario.

Richard Ernest William TURNER, Komati River, 7 November 1900

Richard Turner.

Richard Turner was born on 25 July 1871 in Quebec City, Canada, and worked at his father's grocery and lumber business before joining the militia as a second lieutenant in 1892 and transferring to the Royal Canadian Dragoons for service in South Africa.

For his bravery at the Vet River on 6 May 1900 he was awarded the DSO. Then, at Leliefontein, Komati River, near Belfast, on 7 November 1900, General Smith-Dorrien had forced the Boers out of a strong position, which they attempted to recover after they had been reinforced but they were prevented from doing so by the 84th Battery. On the return march the Royal Canadian Dragoons acted as a rearguard, holding back 200 mounted Boers. Lieutenant Cockburn and Lieutenant Turner, with Sergeant Holland, tried to stop them from capturing two 12-pounder guns. Cockburn and a few men held them off long enough to enable the guns to be got away to safety, Cockburn being wounded at this time. When the Boers again threatened to capture the guns, Holland used his Colt revolver to deadly effect, until finding the enemy almost on top of him. Turner, although twice wounded, then dismounted and deployed some men at close quarters and drove off the Boers.

On his return to Canada after the war, Turner was presented with his VC (gazetted on 23 April 1901) by the Duke of Cornwall & York (later George V) in Quebec on 17 September that year.

By the start of the First World War Turner had been promoted to brigadier general and given command of the 3rd Brigade of the 1st Division, CEF, with Colonel Garnet Hughes as brigade major. Sent to France, his unit came under the first gas attack of the war on 22 April 1915 at Ypres. In the chaos that followed both he and Hughes sent erroneous messages that the line had been broken, when in fact it had not even been attacked. Turner was also responsible for a night attack on

Kitchener's Wood, although he left the details to Hughes, who insisted on an immediate attack before proper reconnaissance could reveal the presence of enfilading machine-gun positions. Although Turner displayed great bravery when his headquarters came under small arms and artillery fire, on the next day he suddenly ordered his brigade to withdraw without informing his commanding officer or the brigade commander on his left flank. After another poor performance in April 1916 at St Eloi, Turner was relieved of his command and moved to administrative duties.

Richard Turner attended the 1956 centenary VC reunion in London. He died on 19 June 1961 and is buried in Mount Hermon Cemetery, Section U, Chemin St Louis, Sillery, Quebec City, Canada. His VC is held by the Royal Canadian Dragoons, Patawawa, Ontario.

Edward James Gibson HOLLAND, Komati River, 7 November 1900

Edward Holland was born on 2 February 1878 in Ottawa, Ontario, Canada, and attended the Lisgar Collegiate Institute. He enlisted into the militia in 1895 and within four years was posted to South Africa with the rank of sergeant.

At Leliefontein, Komati River, near Belfast, on 7 November 1900, General Smith-Dorrien had forced the Boers out of a strong position, which they attempted to recover after they had been reinforced but they were prevented by the 84th Battery. On the return march the Royal Canadian Dragoons acted as a rearguard, holding back 200 mounted Boers. Lieutenant Cockburn and Lieutenant Turner, with Sergeant Holland, tried to stop them from capturing two 12-pounder guns. Cockburn and a few men held them off long enough to enable the guns to be got away to safety, Cockburn being wounded at this time. When the Boers again threatened to capture the guns, Holland used a Colt machine gun mounted on a carriage between the

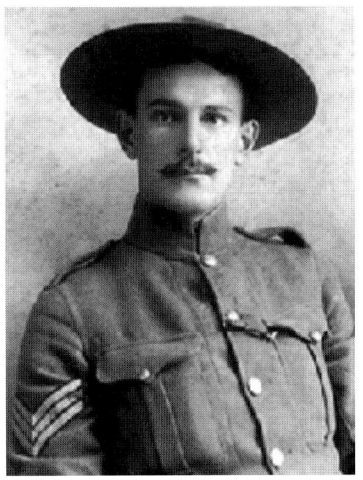

Edward Holland.

two 12-pounder guns to deadly effect, until finding the enemy almost on top of him and the machine gun jammed. As the carriage horse was too exhausted to pull away, Holland retrieved the weapon from the top of the carriage, mounted another horse and galloped away from the Boers with the still hot machine gun under his arm.

Holland's VC was gazetted on 23 April 1901 and presented to him on 20 September that year by the Duke of Cornwall & York (later George V) in Ottawa and he was given a commission. In 1909 he prospected in gold, taking part in the Gillies Limit Rush in 1912. He later held the rank of major and commanded a mounted machine-gun battery in the First World War, returning home as a lieutenant colonel. After the war he sold typewriters and cash registers. He married Dora Knapp and they had two sons and a daughter.

Edward Holland died from a heart attack on 18 June 1948 and his ashes were scattered on Lake Temagami, Ontario, Canada. His VC is held by the Royal Canadian Dragoons, Patawawa, Ontario.

Charles Thomas KENNEDY, Dewetsdorp, 22 November 1900

Charles Kennedy was born on 6 January 1873 in Edinburgh, one of thirteen children, although only four survived to adulthood. He went into the furniture trade but due to the 1891 depression he volunteered for the Highland Light Infantry and in 1894 was posted to India, being part of the Malakand Field Force. Kennedy returned to Scotland in 1898 after his seven years' service was up, and was placed on the Reserve list. When the Boer War broke out he was called back to the colours.

Charles Kennedy.

Kennedy saw action at Magersfontein and in the decisive encircling operation known as Wittebergen, which resulted in large numbers of captured Boers. Now using guerrilla tactics, most regiments were broken into smaller units and Kennedy's company was assigned to Dewetsdorp, about 40 miles south-east of Bloemfontein. When the Boers attacked, capturing a hill overlooking the town, Private Kennedy and six others volunteered to retake the position. Private David McGregor was wounded and bleeding to death. Kennedy went to his assistance and carried him for nearly a mile under heavy fire to the hospital. The following day he volunteered to take a message to the commanding officer across an area under enemy fire. Kennedy was severely wounded after just 20 yards and had to give up.

Following the award of his VC, gazetted on 18 October 1901, and presented to him on 16 December that year by Edward VII at St James's Palace, he was discharged from the army in June 1902 as medically unfit due to his wound.

Charles Kennedy died on 24 April 1907 from injuries received when trying to stop a runaway horse and cart, saving the lives of several children. He is buried in North Merchiston Cemetery, Plot P, Compartment 187, Edinburgh. His VC is held by the Royal Highland Fusiliers Museum, Glasgow.

Donald Dickson FARMER, Nooitgedacht, 13 December 1900

Donald Farmer.

Donald Farmer was born on 28 May 1877 in Kelso, in the Scottish Borders, the son of Thomas and Iona Farmer. At 14 he wanted to join the army but was told he was too young and he should do six weeks with the militia. On hearing the news his father forbade it, telling Donald not to darken his door again if he enlisted. Farmer enlisted into the Queen's Own Cameron Highlanders just short of his fifteenth birthday, giving his age as 18.

In September 1892, after training he was posted to Malta to join the 1st Battalion and three years later was sent to Gibraltar. He was promoted to corporal in 1897 and given home leave. Knowing he could not return to his family home he accepted the offer from fellow soldier Robert Bonnar to stay with his family, where he met Bonnar's sister Helen, whom he later married. In 1898 the two men left for service in the Sudanese campaign, seeing action at Atbara and Khartoum. In January 1900 the battalion was ordered to South Africa; Farmer was by now a sergeant and part of the mounted infantry.

Lord Kitchener sent General Clements to clear the Magaliesberg of Boers, between Pretoria and Rustenburg. He camped at Nooitgedacht, overlooked by the mountains and a nek. At 3.45 am on 13 December 1900, they were attacked by combined commandos in a three-pronged manoeuvre. After they had overrun the British position the Boers attacked the mounted infantry's camp. Lieutenant Sandilands, with fifteen men (including Farmer), went to the assistance of the picquet line, which was heavily engaged, most of them being killed or wounded. Sandilands was wounded in the liver and both shoulders. Farmer went to his assistance and carried him away under a very heavy and close fire to a place of safety and then he returned to the firing line. Farmer then helped to distribute ammunition taken from the dead and wounded to those still able to fight. He was eventually taken prisoner. Three days later, Farmer was able to escape by knocking his guard unconscious and he made his way back to his battalion.

His VC, gazetted on 12 April 1901, was presented to him on 14 August that year by the Duke of Cornwall & York (later George V) at Pietermaritzburg. On his return to Scotland he married Helen Bonnar and they had a son and three daughters. Farmer was promoted to colour sergeant in February 1905 and was later commissioned.

By the summer of 1914, Farmer had served twenty-two years in the army. He was sent to France with the Liverpool Scottish and first saw action at Hooge, where twenty-one out of twenty-three officers and nearly 400 men were killed. In his own words, 'Our Medical Officer was the bravest man I know. He was missing for 2–3 days after the Hooge Battle and it was found that he had attended all the wounded in No Man's Land and had also dressed the wounds of the Huns.' The man in question was none other than Noel Chavasse VC and Bar, MC.

Farmer continued to see service at the front and was reported as missing, presumed dead, causing much distress to his family before it was realised that it was an administrative error. Farmer survived the war and served for a short time during the Second World War in the Home Guard.

Donald Farmer attended the VC centenary celebrations held in 1956. He died on 23 December 1956 and his ashes are interred at Anfield Crematorium, Plot 9, Garden of Remembrance, Priory Road, Liverpool. His VC is held by the Queen's Own Highlanders Museum, Fort George, Ardersier, Inverness-shire.

Chapter 16

Monument Hill, Naauwpoort, Bothwell Camp, Strijdenburg and Derby

John BARRY, Monument Hill, 7/8 January 1901

John Barry was born on 1 February 1873 in Kilkenny, Ireland. Little is known about his life before he enlisted into the 1st Battalion, Royal Irish Regiment in 1890. He served on the North-West Frontier of India and in the Punjab. At the outbreak of the Boer War he was sent to South Africa.

On the night of 7/8 January 1901, General Muller's men effected a complete surprise, overpowered the sentries on Monument Hill, and threw themselves upon the fort. Many were shot down or caught in the wire, but the greater number reached the walls and climbed over them, firing down on the defenders. Heavily outnumbered, Captain George Fosbery and his men fought desperately to the bitter end. In the brief but bloody fight Fosbery fell dead and thirty-nine of his eighty-three men were killed or wounded. One of the Maxim gunners, Private Barry, when all his comrades were down, seized a pick and began to smash the breech of his gun to prevent it from falling into Boer hands. The Boers called on him to stop but he persisted until it was rendered useless. The Boers, robbed of their spoil, shot him dead.

John Barry.

On 8 August 1902, as a result of the award to Lieutenant Frederick Roberts, the policy in the War Office was changed and John Barry was posthumously awarded the VC. He is buried in Belfast Cemetery, East of Johannesburg, South Africa. His VC is in the Ashcroft Gallery, Imperial War Museum, London.

William James HARDHAM, Naauwpoort, 28 January 1901

William Hardham was born on 31 July 1876 in Wellington, New Zealand, the son of George Hardham, of Surrey, England, and his wife Ann (née Gregory). Educated in Wellington and a keen sportsman, William played rugby for the Petone Rugby Club and Wellington Rugby Football Union, eventually playing fifty-three games for the province. He also worked as a blacksmith before joining the cadets in 1891. His military career began in 1894/95 when he joined the Wellington Naval Artillery.

William Hardham

Hardham came to South Africa with the 4th New Zealand Contingent (Rough Riders, an irregular cavalry unit) in April 1900 as a farrier sergeant major. On 28 January 1901, near Naauwpoort, while on patrol his unit was ambushed by about twenty Boers. Although they were able to withdraw, Trooper McCrae was wounded and his horse killed. Farrier Major Hardham rode over to him under heavy fire, dismounted and helped him onto his own horse and then ran alongside until they were out of range.

In March 1901, Hardham's unit was involved in the capture of a convoy of Koos de la Rey's commando. The Rough Riders left for New Zealand in June 1901 and Hardham was discharged two months later. He volunteered for service in South Africa again and in February 1902 was commissioned a lieutenant in the 9th Contingent. But soon after his arrival in South Africa he and fifty others were sent to London to attend the coronation of King Edward VII.

Lieutenant Hardham's VC, gazetted on 4 October 1901, was presented to him by the still uncrowned King Edward on 1 July 1902 at Horse Guards Parade. It would appear that his medal was given to him unengraved and he arranged the engraving himself. He was the first New Zealand-born man to be awarded the VC.

He returned to New Zealand and his work as a blacksmith, and he continued to play rugby until 1910. In 1904 he played against England. Hardham, now a captain, served with the Mounted Rifles at Gallipoli and was wounded in the hand and chest in May 1915. Invalided home, he later became Military Commandant of the Queen Mary Hospital for Sick and Wounded Returned Soldiers in Hanmer Spring, New Zealand. He married Constance Evelyn Parsonson in March 1916. In February 1918 he returned to Europe with reinforcements. He joined the Reserve of Officers in October 1919.

William Hardham died from stomach cancer on 13 April 1928 and is buried in Karori Soldiers' Cemetery, Circle O, Plot 20, Wellington, New Zealand. His VC is held by the National Army Museum, State Highway 1, Waiouru, New Zealand.

William Bernard TRAYNOR, Bothwell Camp, 6 February 1901

William Traynor was born on 31 December 1870 in Hull, Yorkshire, the son of Francis (a hemp dresser) and Rebecca Traynor. He was educated in a Roman Catholic school. He was working as a labourer when he enlisted into the 2nd Battalion, the West Yorkshire Regiment in November 1888 and served in India. He married Jane Martin in June 1897 and they had four sons and two daughters. He was posted to South Africa in October 1899.

William Traynor.

By now a sergeant, Traynor saw action at Colenso, Spion Kop, Vaal Krantz and Pieters Hill. On 6 February 1901, at Bothwell Camp, the Boers, led by General Botha, attacked the camp before dawn and got through two picquet lines. Traynor dashed out of his trench to help a wounded man but was wounded in the chest and thigh. Unable to continue alone, he called for help. Lance Corporal Lintott ran to him and they carried the wounded man to safety. Despite his wounds, Sergeant Traynor remained in command and was most cheerful until the enemy attack failed. Lintott was awarded the DCM.

The War Office mistakenly sent Traynor's wife a telegram informing her that her husband had been 'killed in action'. However, he was alive but his wounds were so bad he was invalided home in March 1901.

Due to his injuries he was unable to travel to London to receive his VC (gazetted on 17 September 1901) from the King, so it was presented to him by Colonel Edward Stevenson Browne VC.

Tryanor served in the First World War on the home front and was mentioned in despatches for 'valuable services in connection with the war'. He was a member of the British Legion in Dover, where he was vice chairman for ten years. In 1951, on the fiftieth anniversary of the award of his VC, the town of Dover honoured him with a civic dinner at the town hall.

Traynor's grave, Charlton Cemetery, Dover, Kent.

William Traynor died on 20 October 1954 and is buried in Charlton Cemetery, Plot XL, Grave 28, Old Charlton Road, Dover, Kent. His VC is in the Ashcroft Gallery, Imperial War Museum, London.

John James CLEMENTS, Strijdenburg, 24 February 1901

John Clements was born on 19 June 1872 in Middleburg, South Africa. He grew up in a farming family prior to his enlistment into Rimington's Guides (a unit of light horse), shortly before the outbreak of the Boer War.

On 24 February 1901, near Strijdenburg, Corporal Clements's patrol ran into some Boers. His commanding officer, Lieutenant Harvey, was mortally wounded and Clements was badly wounded in the lungs. Five Boers came towards him, calling for him to surrender. He jumped up, shot three of them with his revolver, thereby causing all of them to surrender to him and two unwounded men of the Guides.

John Clements.

Clements's VC, gazetted on 4 June 1901, was presented to him on 1 July 1902 by the Prince of Wales (later George V) at Horse Guards Parade,

London. On his return to South Africa he married Florence Palmer and they had five children. He took up farming again but served in Botha's Scouts in the German South West Africa Campaign during the First World War. After the death of his wife in 1917 he remarried and had a further three children.

John Clements died on 18 June 1937 and is buried in Town Cemetery, Dutch Reform Section. Newcastle, South Africa. His VC is in the Ashcroft Gallery, Imperial War Museum, London.

Frederic Brooks DUGDALE, Derby, 3 March 1901

Frederic Dugdale was born on 21 October 1877 in Burnley, Lancashire, the third son of Colonel James Dugdale VD. He was educated at Marlborough College and Christ Church, Oxford before being commissioned second lieutenant in the 5th (Royal Irish) Lancers in October 1899, just prior to the Boer War.

On arrival in South Africa he took part in action at Laing's Nek, the Tugela Heights and the relief of Ladysmith under Sir Redvers Buller VC, and was promoted to lieutenant in May 1900. On 3 March 1901, at Derby, east of Krugersdorp, Transvaal, he was in command of an outpost, having been ordered to retire. His party came under heavy fire from the enemy, wounding a sergeant, two men and a horse. He dismounted and placed a wounded man on his own horse. Catching a riderless horse, he rode over to another casualty, took him up behind him and then brought both men safely out of action.

Lieutenant Dugdale caught enteric fever but regained his health and served under

Frederic Dugdale.

Dugdale's grave, Longborough churchyard, Gloucestershire.

General French in the Cape. He returned to England in July 1902 and was presented with his VC (gazetted on 17 September 1901) on 24 October 1902 by Edward VII.

Tragically, Frederic Dugdale died on 13 November 1902 as a result of injuries sustained after falling from his horse while out hunting. He is buried in Longborough churchyard, Longborough, Gloucestershire. His VC is held by the Queen's Royal Lancers Museum, Belvoir Castle, Grantham, Leicestershire.

Chapter 17

Brakpan, Lambrechtfontein, Thaba 'Nchu, Vlakfontein, Springbok Laagte, Ruiter's Kraal, Blood River, Itala, Moedwil, Geelhoutboom, Tygerkloof Spruit, Tafelkop and Vlakfontein

Frederick William BELL, Brakpan, 16 May 1901

Frederick Bell was born on 3 April 1875 in Perth, Western Australia, the son of Henry Thomas Bell, a clerk, and Alice Agnes (née Watson). He was educated at A.D. Letch's Preparatory School and at the government school, Perth. He joined the Western Public Service in November 1894 as a cadet in the Department of Customs, where he later became a cashier.

On the outbreak of the Boer War, Bell enlisted into the West Australian (Mounted Infantry) Contingent. He first saw action at Slingersfontein, then took part in the relief of Johannesburg and of Pretoria, and the

Frederick Bell.

Battles of Diamond Hill and Wittebergen. At Palmietfontein he was badly wounded and invalided to England. On his return to Perth in February 1901, Bell was commissioned a lieutenant in the 6th Contingent and set sail for South Africa in March.

On 16 May that year, at Brakpan, while retreating under heavy fire after holding the flank, Lieutenant Bell noticed a dismounted trooper. He took the man behind him on his horse but the weight was too much for the animal and it fell. Bell ordered the trooper to save himself and he remained behind to fire on the pursuing Boers until his comrade was out of danger.

After his discharge in May 1902, Bell joined the Australian section of the coronation escort for King Edward VII. He was presented his VC (gazetted on 4 June 1901) by the Prince of Wales (later George V) on 1 July 1902 at Horse Guards Parade, London.

After briefly returning to Perth, he came back to England in 1905, joined the Colonial Service and was appointed to British Somaliland as an assistant district officer. Made an assistant political officer later that year, he held the post until 1910. While in Somaliland he took up big game hunting but was badly mauled by a lion. Bell was assistant resident in Nigeria 1910–12 and from then until the outbreak of the First World War he was an assistant commissioner in Kenya.

Bell's grave, Canford Cemetery, Bristol.

Bell served in France with the Royal Irish Dragoon Guards. He was mentioned in despatches and promoted to captain in 1915 and then to major, and later became a lieutenant colonel, and commanded a rest camp and an embarkation camp in England. After the war he returned to the Colonial Service in Kenya, married Mabel Mackenzie Valentini (née Skinner) and in 1925 went into retirement in England. During the Second World War he was in the Reserve of Officers. After his wife died in 1944 he married Brenda Margaret Cracklow (née Illingworth). Neither of his marriages produced any children.

Frederick Bell died on 28 April 1954 and is buried in Canford Cemetery, Section O, Colour Pink, Grave 126, Canford Lane, Bristol. His VC is held by the Western Australia Museum, Perth, Western Australia.

Gustavus Hamilton Blenkinsopp COULSON, Lambrechtfontein, 18 May 1901

Gustavus Coulson was born on 1 April 1879 in Wimbledon, London, the only son of H.J.W. Coulson and great-grandson of Colonel Blenkinsopp Coulson. He joined 4th Battalion (Princess of Wales's Own) Yorkshire Regiment, but transferred to the King's Own Scottish Borderers. In January 1900 his regiment was posted to South Africa.

Lieutenant Coulson had a horse shot from under him during the charge at the Battle of Paardeberg, where Colonel Hannay fell. He stayed out, shooting Boers who came to steal the saddles of the fallen. Afterwards he took part in the advance on Pretoria and was present at the surrender of General Prinsloo, in the Brandwater Basin, in July 1900, and later saw action near Bothaville, where Lieutenant Colonel Le Gallais fell. For his gallantry in the campaign of 1900, Coulson was awarded the DSO, gazetted on 27 September 1901.

Gustavus Coulson.

On 18 May 1901, near Lambrechtfontein, during a rearguard action he saw Corporal Cranmer's horse had fallen. He took the corporal onto his own horse but it was shot and both men fell. With the enemy rapidly approaching he ordered Cranmer to ride the wounded horse away as best he could. Corporal Shaw, seeing Coulson in danger, came to his aid, taking him upon his horse, but almost at once both men were shot dead. Shaw was awarded the DCM.

Gustavus Coulson is buried at Lambrechtfontein Farm, near Bothaville, South Africa. His VC is held by the King's Own Scottish Borderers Museum, Berwick-upon-Tweed, Northumberland.

James ROGERS, Thaba 'Nchu, 15 June 1901

James Rogers was born on 4 July 1873 in Moama, NSW, Australia, the son of Welsh-born John Rogers, a farmer, and his wife Sarah Louisa (née Johnstone), of Sydney. He was educated locally at public schools. In 1886 his family moved to Heywood, Victoria, where he worked on his father's farm and enlisted into the Victorian Mounted Rifles in 1898.

James Rogers.

Rogers sailed to South Africa with his unit in November 1899 and the following May was seconded to the Provincial Mounted Police as a corporal. When the Victorian contingent returned home in November 1900, Rogers joined the South African Constabulary as a sergeant. In June, a column of the Royal Irish Rifles were active between Thaba 'Nchu and Tabaksberg in search of Boer forces. On 15 June 1901 they came under sniper fire near Thaba 'Nchu. Lieutenant F. Dickinson, Sergeant Rogers and six men of the South African Constabulary formed a rearguard and surprised sixty Boers. As the men withdrew, Dickinson's horse was shot. Rogers rode back, lifted him onto his own horse and rode with him for half a mile to cover. He then went back to within 400 yards of the enemy to rescue two more men who had lost their horses. Finally he captured two riderless horses and helped their riders to mount and escape, all under a very heavy fire.

Rogers returned to Australia in December 1901. His VC was gazetted on 18 April 1902 and it was presented to him on 18 September that year by the Governor General of Australia, Lord Tennyson, in Melbourne. A month later, he returned to South Africa, but the war was over by the time he arrived and his battalion was sent home. Rogers again returned to South Africa and joined the Cape Town Police, serving until 1907, when he left for Australia. That same year, he married Ethel Maud Seldon and they had two sons. By 1912 he was a maker at Williamstown rifle range and by the outbreak of the First World War, he was an assistant ranger. On 6 December 1914, Rogers was commissioned a lieutenant in the 3rd Light Horse Brigade Train, Australian Army Service Corps. He was seriously wounded at Gallipoli in August 1915 and evacuated to Egypt. He then served with the ANZAC Provost Corps before returning home in July 1918.

Rogers resumed work at Williamstown as an assistant ranger, then in 1921 became an assistant storeman, Ordnance Branch, AMF, Victoria, but resigned the following year to take up farming. Rogers and his wife attended the Victoria Cross Centenary ceremony in London in 1956.

He lived at Kew, Melbourne, for more than thirty years, then, after his wife died, he moved to Sydney with his one surviving son.

James Rogers died on 28 October 1961 and was cremated at Springvale Crematorium, Melbourne, Victoria, Australia, where his ashes are in an urn in the columbarium. His VC is on display at the Australian War Memorial, Canberra.

William John ENGLISH, Vlakfontein, 3 July 1901

William English was born on 6 October 1882 in Cork, Ireland, the son of Major William English OBE. He was educated at Harvey Grammar School in Folkestone, Kent, 1894–98, and Campbell College, Belfast, 1898–99. English signed on with the Merchant Navy and sailed to South Africa. Once there he volunteered for service with the 2nd Scottish Horse, which was raised by the Earl of Tullibardine in South Africa, and he was commissioned a lieutenant in March 1901.

William English.

On 3 July 1901 at Vlakfontein, English, with five others, was holding a position on the right during an attack by the Boers. Two of the men were killed and two wounded, but the position held, largely due to Lieutenant English's personal pluck. As ammunition ran short, he crossed 15 yards of open ground to get a fresh supply, all the time under fire from the enemy, who were only 30 yards away.

After the war he returned to England, where on 1 July 1902 he was presented with his VC (gazetted on 4 June 1901) by the Prince of Wales (later George V) at Horse Guards Parade, London. English joined the Army Service Corps and served with them throughout the First World War. After the death of his first wife, he married Mary Pyper in 1922 and they had two sons. After his retirement from the Indian Service Corps in 1930 he lived in Belfast. During the Second World War he commanded a battalion of the Royal Irish Rifles with the rank of lieutenant colonel and was transferred to the Middle East in 1941.

William English died from a cerebral haemorrhage on 4 July 1941 while on board ship. He is buried in Maala Christian Cemetery, Row I, Grave 21, Yemen. His VC was bequeathed to his former school, Campbell College, and has been on loan to the Imperial War Museum, London. It was due to return to his school in 2020.

Henry 'Harry' George CRANDON, Springbok Laagte, 4 July 1901

Henry Crandon was born on 12 February 1874 in Wells, Somerset, the son of William Crandon and Ellen (née Hewlett). He enlisted into the 18th (Queen Mary's Own) Hussars in 1893 and the following year was posted to India. After five years' service there his regiment was transferred to South Africa in time for the outbreak of the Boer War.

Crandon saw action at Ladysmith during the siege and in most of the major campaigns of the war. On 4 July 1901 at Springbok Laagte, near Ermelo, Privates Berry and Crandon were on patrol and came across a party of Boers, who opened fire on them. Berry was wounded in two places and his horse was killed. Crandon, despite being wounded himself in the right and left shoulder, rode back to Berry's assistance, dismounted and gave him his horse. He then followed him on foot for over 1,000 yards under fire, until they reached cover.

Henry Crandon.

Crandon's VC, gazetted on 18 October 1901, was presented to him on 8 June 1902 by Lord Kitchener at Pretoria, and he was promoted to corporal. After the war he worked as a gardener for Sir Lees Knowles. In 1914, Crandon re-enlisted into the 18th Hussars and was wounded in the foot at Ypres in May 1915. After his recovery he spent two years in the Balkans before moving to Egypt.

Little is known about his life after the First World War other than that he lived in Swinton, Manchester.

Harry Crandon died on 2 January 1953 and is buried in Swinton Cemetery; C of E Section A, Grave 3207 (his headstone has the name Henry), Cemetery Road, South Swinton, Manchester. His VC is not publicly held.

Alexander YOUNG, Ruiter's Kraal, 13 August 1901

Alexander Young was born on 27 January 1873 in Clarinbridge, County Galway, Ireland, the son of William and Annie Young. He was educated at Model School, Galway. In May 1890 he joined the Queen's Bays at Renmore, where his horsemanship brought him to attention. Young served in India and became a riding instructor. He first saw action in the Sudanese Campaign under Kitchener in 1898. He then returned to England and was transferred from there to the Cape Police as an instructor.

On 13 August 1901, at Ruiter's Kraal, towards the close of the action, Sergeant Major Young, with a handful of men, rushed

Alexander Young.

some kopjes that were being held by about twenty Boers. On reaching the objective, the Boers galloped back to another kopje. Young then galloped on for 50 yards ahead of his men and, closing with the enemy, shot one of them and captured Commandant Erasmus, the latter firing three times at point-blank range before being taken prisoner.

Young's VC was gazetted on 18 November 1901, and presented to him on 8 August 1902 by the General Officer Commanding, Cape Colony. After the war he stayed on with the Cape Police. He was involved in the Herero Rebellion in German South West Africa, receiving an award from the Kaiser. However, he publicly burnt the award on the outbreak of the First World War. In 1906 Young served in the Zululand Rebellion, where he was wounded in the face, after which he took up farming in Natal.

On the outbreak of the First World War, Young re-enlisted into the Cape Mounted Police and saw service in German East Africa. After the victory there Young volunteered for service in France. He fought in the 1916 Battle of the Somme and was wounded. After his recovery, Alexander Young was sent back to the Somme and was killed in action on 19 October 1916. He has no known grave, but he is named on the Thiepval Memorial to the missing, Pier 4, Face C. His VC is in the Ashcroft Gallery, Imperial War Museum, London.

Llewelyn Alberic Emilius PRICE-DAVIES, Blood River Poort, 17 September 1901

Llewelyn Price-Davies was born on 30 June 1878 in Chirbury, Shropshire, the third son of Lewis Richard Price. He was educated at Marlborough College and the Royal Military College, Sandhurst. Price-Davies enlisted into the King's Royal Rifle Corps in February 1898 and within a year was posted to South Africa for service in the Boer War.

On 17 September 1901, at Blood River Poort, General Gough attacked a Boer encampment, only to find some 400 mounted Boers emerging from the Poort. This was the vanguard of General Botha's invasion of Natal. As the Boers overwhelmed the right of the British column, hundreds of them were galloping around the flank and rear of the guns, riding up to the drivers (who were trying to get the guns

Llewelyn Price-Davies.

away) and calling on them to surrender. Hearing an order to fire upon the Boers, Lieutenant Price-Davies at once drew his revolver and dashed in among them, in what seemed to be almost certain death (without a moment's hesitation); he was immediately shot and knocked off his horse, but survived. Six officers and thirty-eight men were killed or wounded, while six officers and 235 men were taken prisoner.

Price-Davies's VC, gazetted on 29 November 1901, was presented to him on 8 June 1902 by Lord Kitchener in Pretoria. He had been promoted to captain, in January that year. In 1906 he married Eileen Wilson. From March to July 1906 he was Adjutant and Quartermaster, Mounted Infantry, Irish Command, and from October 1906 to November 1907 he was Adjutant of the 5th Battalion, Mounted Infantry, South Africa. He was a student at the Staff College, Camberley, from 1908 to 1909, and then from November 1901 to June 1912 was Brigade Major, 13th Brigade, Irish Command. He was then appointed to the War Office from 1912 to 1914.

Price-Davies was promoted to major in 1915 and commanded a brigade in England, before embarking for France and the Western Front, seeing service there until November 1917. He returned home with the brevet rank of lieutenant colonel. Created a CMG in 1918, he was given a special deployment in Italy with the rank of major general. From 1920 to 1930, he was ADC to the King, and from 1920 to 1924, Assistant Adjutant General at Aldershot, and commander of the 145th Infantry Brigade until 1927. He was Quartermaster General in Gibraltar until 1930, and from 1933 to 1948, a Member of the Honourable Corps of Gentlemen-at-Arms. During the Second World War he commanded a battalion in the Home Guard from 1940 to 1945.

Llewelyn Price-Davies died on 26 December 1965 and is buried in St Andrew's churchyard, High Street, Sonning, Berkshire. His VC is held by the Royal Green Jackets Museum, Winchester, Hampshire.

Price-Davies's grave, St Andrew's churchyard, Sonning, Berkshire.

Frederick Henry BRADLEY, Itala, 26 September 1901

Frederick Bradley was born on 27 September 1876 in London, the son of Edward Thomas Bradley. At 16 he enlisted into the 69th Battery, Royal Field Artillery as a driver and was posted to South Africa for service in the Boer War.

He was present in a number of actions, including Talana, the defence of Ladysmith and Laing's Nek. Then, in September 1901, General Botha invaded Natal and attacked the Itala garrison with 1,600 men. The British, mostly mounted infantry, held on for sixteen hours. During the action Major

Frederick Bradley.

Chapman called for volunteers to carry ammunition up the hill; Driver Lancashire and Gunner Bull at once came forward and started to cross 150 yards of open ground under fire. Halfway across, Lancashire fell wounded; Driver Bradley and Bull, without a moment's hesitation, ran out and caught Lancashire up, and Gunner Rabb carried him to a place of safety. Then Bradley, with the aid of Gunner Boddy, succeeded in getting the ammunition up the hill. Lancashire, Bull, Rabb and Boddy were all awarded the DCM.

Bradley's VC was gazetted on 27 December 1901 and was presented to him on 8 June 1902 by Lord Kitchener in Pretoria. He was promoted to bombardier. He remained in South Africa after the war and took part in the Zulu Rebellion of 1906 as a mounted machine-gunner with the Transvaal Mounted Rifles. He continued to serve in South African units and narrowly survived a railway collision during the campaign in German South West Africa during the First World War. Transferring to the British Army, he was commissioned captain and commanded six batteries of mortars on the Somme until wounded near Delville Wood in November 1916.

He returned to South Africa and continued to serve in local units, finally retiring, as a major, to run a pub in Zululand. A modest man, he declined the £10 annuity given to recipients of the VC, insisting instead that it be sent to the Royal Hospital Chelsea, home of the Chelsea Pensioners.

Frederick Bradley died on 10 March 1943 following an operation and is buried in Gwelo Cemetery, Grave 971, Gwelo, Zimbabwe. His VC is in the Ashcroft Gallery, Imperial War Museum, London.

William Dolman BEES, Moedwil, 30 September 1901

William Bees was born on 12 September 1871 in Midsomer Norton, Somerset, the son of William and Jane Bees. He was educated at the Board School and joined the 1st Battalion, Derbyshire Regiment (later the Sherwood Foresters) in March 1870, seeing service on the North-West Frontier in 1897–98, taking part in the Tirah campaign, after which he was posted to South Africa.

In the Western Transvaal, General Kekewich's column was camped at Moedwil, on the banks of the Selons River, between Rustenburg and Zeerust. At 4.45 am on 30 September 1901, they were attacked by General De la Rey, the Boers gaining the crest of a nearby hill and firing into the camp. General Kekewich was hit twice and the gunners suffered severely. Six out of nine men (including Captains Keller and Baldwin) attached to a Maxim gun were wounded. Unable to bear the cries of the wounded any longer, Private Bees dashed forward under heavy fire to a spruit 500 yards ahead of the gun, filled his camp kettle and returned to quench the men's thirsts. The kettle was hit by several bullets during his dash, but he was unharmed. The Boer attack was repulsed when Kekewich used the Scottish Horse in a flanking movement. Bees was promoted to corporal on the field of battle. British casualties were 214 men and the Boers were about 60.

William Bees.

Corporal Bees's VC was gazetted on 17 December 1901 and was presented to him on 30 July 1902 by Lord Kitchener at Pretoria. In September that year he was discharged from service. On 25 April 1903 he married Sarah Freeman and they had a son and a daughter. His best man was Harry Beet VC.

Bees joined the army in October 1914 but was discharged due to illness. After his recovery he enlisted again in April 1915 into the Sherwood Foresters and was based at Whitburn, near Sunderland, until transferred into the Durham Light Infantry at Blythe and South Shields. After a year, he was then transferred to Class W for mining. Bees re-enlisted yet again, into the Royal Army Service Corps in January 1918, and was transferred to the Army Reserve following demobilisation in February 1918.

William Bees lived the majority of his remaining life in Leicestershire, where he died on 20 June 1938. He is buried in London Road Cemetery, Grave 3040, London Road, Coalville, Leicestershire. His VC is held by the Sherwood Foresters Museum, The Castle, Nottingham.

Leslie 'Elsie' Cecil MAYGAR, Geelhoutboom, 23 November 1901

Leslie Maygar was born on 27 May 1868 in Dean Station, Kilmore, Victoria, Australia, the son of a grazier who emigrated from England with his wife. His father's family were originally political refugees from Hungary. He was educated at Kilmore State School and then privately. A fine horseman, Maygar enlisted into the Victorian Mounted Rifles in March 1891 and was commissioned in July 1900. He was not accepted at first for service in South Africa due to a decayed tooth, but went with the 5th Victorian Mounted Rifles, arriving in Cape Town in March 1901.

Leslie Maygar.

For twelve months his unit was constantly in action, north of Middleburg, the East Transvaal, Rhenoster Kop, Klippan, Koornfontein and Drivelfontein, before being transferred to Natal in August. Then he took part in an engagement at Geelhoutboom on 23 November 1901. Lieutenant Maygar went to order the retirement of a detachment that was being outflanked. As the retired Trooper A. Short had his horse shot from under him, Maygar dismounted and lifted him onto his own horse. The animal, not up to carrying both of them, bolted into a swamp. Maygar ordered the man to ride to safety while he made his way back on foot. He was under heavy fire the whole time.

His VC, gazetted on 11 February 1902, was presented to him on 8 June 1902 by Lord Kitchener at Pretoria. Maygar stayed on in South Africa for the remainder of the war. On his return to Australia he took up work as a grazier but also served in the 8th (later 16th) Light Horse and was promoted to captain in 1905.

Maygar enlisted on the outbreak of the First World War, and was appointed captain in the 4th Light Horse, sailing for Egypt in October 1915. In Gallipoli he was promoted to major and given temporary command of the 8th Light Horse, both the rank of lieutenant colonel and the command being confirmed in December. During the evacuation he was left in command of forty men and told to hold the trenches at all cost. He wrote: 'I had my usual good luck to be given command of the last party to pull out of the trenches, the post of honour for the 3rd Light Horse Brigade.'

Maygar led his regiment throughout its service in Sinai and Palestine until he was wounded by an aeroplane bomb at Beersheba on 31 October 1917. His arm was amputated and he appeared to be recovering, but on 17 November his wound started to haemorrhage and he died in the hospital at Karm, Palestine.

Leslie Maygar is buried in Beersheba War Cemetery, Row Q, Grave 82, Beersheba, Israel. His VC is on display at the Australian War Memorial, Canberra.

Thomas Joseph CREAN, Tygerkloof Spruit, 18 December 1901

Thomas Crean was born on 19 April 1873 in Dublin, Ireland, the fifth child of Michael Theobald Crean, a barrister, and his wife Emma. He was educated at Belvedere College, Dublin, and Clongowes Wood College, Co Kildare. Crean was an excellent athlete and a strong swimmer. In September 1891, while swimming he saved the life of another student, Wm Ahern, from drowning, off Blackrock, Co Dublin, and was awarded the Royal Humane Society's medal for life-saving at sea.

Crean studied medicine from 1891 and graduated in 1896. He played rugby for his college and represented Leinster from 1894 to 1896. In 1896, Crean was a member of the British Lions squad for their tour of South Africa, playing in three of the four tests against South Africa. After the tour ended he and Robert Johnston (who would also go on to be awarded the VC, see Chapter 2) decided to stay on and played rugby for the Transvaal. At the start of the Boer War in 1899, Crean and Johnston enlisted into the Imperial Light Horse and served through the defence of Ladysmith, and Crean was appointed captain. In 1901 he became Brigade Medical Officer with the rank of surgeon captain.

Thomas Crean.

After the third drive to capture the Boer commander Christiaan de Wet, General Dartnell's column was returning to Harrismith when they were ambushed by de Wet's commandos at Tygerkloof Spruit on 18 December 1901. Crean, under heavy fire, tended to the wounded in the firing line, despite being wounded himself and only 150 yards from the enemy. He only stopped when he was wounded for the second time. Crean's wounds were so serious that he was not at first expected to live. The Boers were eventually driven off.

Due to his severe stomach and arm wounds, and despite his protests, he was invalided back to England. His VC, gazetted on 11 February 1902, was presented to him on 13 March 1902 by Edward VII at St James's Palace. He married Victoria Heredia in 1905 and they had two children. Crean continued to serve with the RAMC until 1906, when he took up a private practice in Harley Street.

At the start of the First World War he re-joined the RAMC and served with the 1st Cavalry Brigade. He was wounded several times, mentioned in despatches and

Crean's grave, St Mary's RC Cemetery, Kensal Rise, London.

awarded the DSO. In 1916 he was promoted to major and commanded the 44th Field Ambulance.

After the war he struggled to carry on with his practice (which had been worth £3,000 a year) due to the stress from his war service. In 1920 he went to money lenders, who charged him £675 in interest, and by 1922 he was bankrupt.

Thomas Crean died from diabetes on 25 March 1923 and is buried in St Mary's RC Cemetery, Grave 896, Harrow Road, Kensal Rise, London. His VC is on display at the Museum of Military Medicine, Keogh Barracks, Aldershot, Surrey.

Alfred Ernest IND, Tafelkop, 20 December 1901

Alfred Ind was born on 16 September 1872 in Tetbury, Gloucestershire, the son of George Ind. Nothing is known of his early life before enlisting into the Royal Field Artillery in February 1891, aged 19, as a shoeing smith with a troop of pom-pom guns. At the outbreak of the Boer War he was soon en route to South Africa.

While operating south-east of Frankfort on the Wilge River, General Damant's force became separated from Rimington. On 20 December 1901, Damant's small force was attacked by 300 Boers of the Vrede Commando near Tafelkop. In the action that followed

Alfred Ind.

most of the gunners were shot down around their guns, Damant being hit four times. Ind continued to fire into the advancing Boers until the last possible moment. Captain Jeffcoat, who was mortally wounded in this action, requested that Shoeing-Smith Ind's gallant conduct on this and in every other action since he joined the pom-pom service be brought to notice. They were eventually relieved by Rimington, but suffered 33 killed and 45 wounded out of 90 men. Ind was mentioned in despatches and promoted to corporal. In later service he was wounded and four times mentioned in despatches.

His VC, gazetted on 15 August 1902, was presented to him on 20 November 1902 by Edward VII at Buckingham Palace. He was later a member of the celebrated battery known as the Chestnut Troop. From 1911 he served as a lodge keeper to the 2nd Duke of Westminster at Eaton Hall, Cheshire.

Alfred Ind died on 29 November 1916 and is buried in St Mary the Virgin Churchyard, Church Road, Eccleston, Cheshire. His VC was sold in 1920 and is not publicly held.

Ind's grave, St Mary the Virgin Churchyard, Eccleston, Cheshire.

Arthur MARTIN-LEAKE, Vlakfontein, 8 February 1902 & Bar, Zonnebeke, Belgium, 29 October to 8 November 1914

Arthur Martin-Leake was born on 4 April 1874 at the family home 'Marshalls', High Cross, near Ware, Hertfordshire, the fifth of eight children born to Stephen Martin-Leake. He was educated at Westminster School and the University College, qualifying in medicine in 1898. His first appointment was at a district hospital in Hemel Hempstead. This was short-lived; as soon as the Boer War broke out he enlisted into the Hertfordshire Yeomanry as a trooper.

Martin-Leake remained with this unit throughout its first year in service in South Africa, taking part in several important engagements, notably Prineeloo's surrender and the relief of Hoar's Laager. When his unit returned to England, Martin-Leake remained behind and was employed by the army as a civil surgeon. When General Baden-Powell formed the South African Constabulary he joined with the rank of surgeon captain.

Arthur Martin-Leake.

Geelhoutboom, Tygerkloof Spruit, Tafelkop and Vlakfontein

When a line of posts held by the South African Constabulary was to be extended near Vlakfontein, a reconnaissance party of 130 men under Captain Capell found themselves within 400 yards of a Boer laager, which attacked with superior numbers. Sergeant Waller was hit in the leg and Martin-Leake risked his life to tend to him, going 100 yards into open ground under fire from forty Boers. Later, while attending to the mortally wounded Lieutenant Abraham, he was wounded three times himself, but gave up his efforts only when completely exhausted, and then he refused water until all the other wounded had been attended to.

The Boers then rushed the position and took the remaining men prisoner. They expressed regret at having shot Martin-Leake but said that, as he dashed from one man to another, they did not realise he was attending to their wounds. After his release he was recommended for the VC by Baden-Powell, and it was gazetted on 13 May 1902.

His VC was presented to him on 2 June 1902 by Edward VII at St James's Palace. Martin-Leake returned to the medical profession as soon as he was able and, having passed his examinations, was admitted as a Fellow to the Royal College of Surgeons in June 1903. In the autumn of 1903 he took up a position in India as Administrative Medical Officer of the Bengal-Nagpur Railway, an appointment he held until 1912. He returned to England on leave; while there, the Balkan War broke out and he served with the Red Cross of Montenegro and was decorated by King Nicholas.

Back in India, the news broke that war with Germany had been declared and, after obtaining a leave of absence from the Bengal-Nagpur Railway, Martin-Leake made his way to England. He only got as far as France, where he joined the 5th Field Ambulance, 2nd Division, Royal Army Medical Corps, with the rank of lieutenant.

At Zonnebeke, Belgium, from 29 October to 8 November 1914, he showed conspicuous bravery and devotion to duty in rescuing a large number of wounded men who were lying close to the enemy trenches while exposed to heavy fire. His citation reads in part: 'Lieutenant Arthur Martin-Leake who was awarded the VC on 13 May 1902 is granted a clasp for conspicuous bravery in the present campaign'.

He was presented with his Bar, gazetted on 18 February 1915 (becoming the first of only three men to be awarded the VC twice), on 24

July 1915 by George V at Windsor Castle. He was promoted to captain, and then to major in November 1915. After a brief period back in the Balkans with the Adriatic Mission, he commanded a Field Ambulance, being promoted to temporary lieutenant colonel in April 1917, and later a casualty clearing station with the 1st Army. At the end of his contract in September 1918 he took leave in England before returning to India to work for the Bengal-Nagpur Railway. Martin-Leake retired to England in 1937, living at the family home.

On the outbreak of the Second World War he again saw service, this time with a mobile medical unit. In retirement he enjoyed riding his motorbike and flying his own aircraft, as well as gardening and cooking. Arthur Martin-Leake died from lung cancer on 22 June 1953 and his ashes are interred at St John the Evangelist churchyard, High Cross, near Ware, Hertfordshire. His VC and BAR are on display at the Museum of Military Medicine, Keogh Barracks, Aldershot, Surrey.

The other two men to be awarded the VC and BAR are Noel Chavasse and Charles Upham. There is another link between these men: Martin-Leake was serving with the 46th Field Ambulance, which brought Chavasse back to Brandhoeck, and Upham was a distant relation to Chavasse by marriage.

Martin-Leake's memorial stone, St John the Evangelist churchyard, High Cross, near Ware, Hertfordshire, where his ashes are interred.

Glossary

assegai	long-bladed stabbing spear
brevet	an honorary or temporary promotion
colitis	inflammation of the gastrointestinal system
donga	a deep gully or ravine
forlorn hope	a suicidal assault
grazier	large-scale sheep or cattle farmer
Kaffir	a black African, a term now considered to be an insult
kop	hill
kopje (also koppie)	small hill
kraal	an enclosure for cattle or sheep
laager	encampment with fortified perimeter, sometimes with wagons
Legion d'Honneur	the highest military award of France, also awarded to civilians and for political reasons
loophole	small holes in a prepared position allowing defenders to fire with little risk to themselves
nek	mountain pass
piquet	soldier or small group of soldiers performing a particular duty, such as being sent out to watch for the enemy
pom-pom	lightweight quick-firing cannons
pont	flat-bottomed ferry worked on cables or ropes.
sangar	a small protected structure from which to fire on the enemy
singlestick	a martial art that uses a wooden stick as a weapon
spruit	small stream or watercourse
wadi	dried-up riverbed

Acronyms and Abbreviations

ADC	Aide-de-Camp
ANZAC	Australian and New Zealand Army Corps
BA	Bachelor of Arts
BEF	British Expeditionary Force
CEF	Canadian Expeditionary Force
C-in-C	Commander-in-Chief
CMG	Companion of the Order of St Michael & George
DCM	Distinguished Conduct Medal
DL	Deputy Lieutenant
DSM	Distinguished Service Medal
DSO	Distinguished Service Order
GOC	General Officer Commanding
JP	Justice of the Peace
MM	Military Medal
NNC	Natal Native Contingent
NSW	New South Wales
POW	prisoner of war
RAMC	Royal Army Medical Corps
RE	Royal Engineers
RFC	Royal Flying Corps
RHA	Royal Horse Artillery
OBE	Order of the British Empire
VD	Volunteer Officers' Decoration
WIA	wounded in action

Bibliography

Bancroft, James, W., *The Zulu War VCs* (James W. Bancroft, 1982)
Barthrop, Michael, *The Zulu War* (Blandford, London, 1992)
Beckett, Ian, *The Victorians at War* (Hambledon & London, 2003)
Brazier, Kevin, *The Complete Victoria Cross* (Pen & Sword, 2020)
Churchill, Winston, *My Early Life* (The Reprint Society, 1930)
Clayton, Ann, *Martin-Leake Double VC* (Leo Cooper, 1994)
Creagh, Sir O'Moore, VC & Humphris, E.M. (eds), *The Victoria Cross 1856–1920* (J.B. Hayward & Son, 1975)
Crook, M.J., *The Evolution of the Victoria Cross* (Midas Books, 1975)
Emery, Frank, *The Red Soldier* (Hodder & Stoughton, 1977)
Holme, Norman, *The Noble 24th* (Savannah Publications, 1999)
Ingleton, Roy, *Kent VCs* (Pen & Sword, 2011)
Johnson, Barry C., *Hook of Rorke's Drift* (Bartletts Press, 2004)
Knight, James, *Marching to the Drums* (Greenhill Books, 2000)
Lloyd, W.G., *John Williams VC* (W.G. Lloyd, 1993)
Manning, Stephen, *Evelyn Wood: Pillar of Empire* (Pen & Sword, 2007)
Pakenham, Thomas, *The Boer War* (Weidenfeld & Nicolson, 1979)
Regan, Geoffrey, *Great Military Blunders* (André Deutsch, 2012)
Symons, Julian, *Buller's Campaign* (White Lion Publishing, 1963)
Thornton, Neil, *Rorke's Drift: A New Perspective* (Fonthill Media, 2016)
Uys, Ian S., *Victoria Crosses of the Anglo-Boer War* (Fortress Financial Group Ltd., 2000)
Uys, Ian S., *The History of Southern Africa's Victoria Cross Heroes* (Uys Publishers, 1973)
Wessels, André (ed), *Lord Kitchener and the War in South Africa 1899–1902* (Sutton Publishing, 2006)
Whitehouse, Howard, *Battle in Africa* (Field Books, 1987)
Williams, Alister, *Commandant of the Transvaal: The Life and Career of General Sir Hugh Rowlands VC, KCB* (Bridge Books, 2001)
Wilson, H.W., *With the Flag to Pretoria* (Harmsworth Bros Ltd., 1900)
Wilson, H.W., *After Pretoria: The Guerrilla War* (Harmsworth Bros Ltd., 1900)

Alphabetical List

ALBRECHT, Herman	99
ALLAN (ALLEN), William	16
ATKINSON, Alfred	105
BABTIE, William	94
BARRY, John	149
BEES, William Dolman	165
BEET, Harry Churchill	121
BELL, Frederick William	155
BERESFORD, William Leslie de la Poer	54
BISDEE, John Hutton	138
BOOTH, Anthony Clarke	39
BRADLEY, Frederick Henry	164
BROMHEAD, Gonville	13
BROWN (later BROWN-SYNGE-HUTCHINSON, Edward Douglas	140
BROWNE, Edward Stevenson	52
BULLER, Redvers Henry	41
CHARD, John Rouse Merriott	9
CLEMENTS, John James	152
COCKBURN, Hampden Zane Churchill	142
COGHILL, Nevill Josiah Aylmer	5
CONGREVE, Walter Norris	87
COULSON, Gustavus Hamilton Blenkinsopp	157
CRANDON, Henry George	160
CREAN, Thomas Joseph	167
CURTIS, Albert Edward	107

DALTON, James Langley	34
DANAHER, John	62
D'ARCY, Henry Cecil Dudgeon	56
DIGBY-JONES, Robert James Thomas	99
DOOGAN, John	64
DOUGLAS, Henry Edward Manning	83
DOXAT, Alexis Charles	141
DUGDALE, Frederic Brooks	153
DURRANT, Alfred Edward	136
ENGLEHEART, Henry William	112
ENGLISH, William John	159
FARMER, Donald Dickson	147
FARMER, Joseph John	66
FIRTH, James	108
FITZCLARENCE, Charles	71
FOWLER, Edmund John	50
GLASOCK, Horace Henry	116
GORDON, William Eagleson	126
HAMPTON, Harry	133
HARDHAM, William James	150
HEATON, William Edward	135
HILL (later HILL-WALKER), Alan Richard	63
HITCH, Frederick	18
HOLLAND, Edward James Gibson	145
HOOK, Alfred Henry	20
HOUSE, William John	131
HOWSE, Neville Reginald	128
IND, Alfred Ernest	169
INKSON, Edgar Thomas	109
JOHNSTON, Robert	73
JONES, Robert	23
JONES, William	25

KENNEDY, Charles Thomas 146
KIRBY, Frank Howard 123
KNIGHT, Henry James 134

LAWRENCE, Brian Turner Tom 132
LEET, William Knox 46
LODGE, Isaac 116
LYSONS, Henry 48

MACKAY, John Frederick 122
MANSEL-JONES, Conwyn 110
MARTINEAU, Horace Robert 80
MARTIN-LEAKE, Arthur 170
MASTERSON, James Edward Ignatius 100
MAYGAR, Leslie Cecil 166
MAXWELL, Francis Aylmer 117
MEIKLEJOHN, Matthew Fontaine Maury 76
MELVILL, Teignmouth 3
MILBANKE, John Peniston 98
MULLINS, Charles Hubert 75
MURRAY, James 61

NICKERSON, William Henry Snyder 120
NORWOOD, John 79
NURSE, George Edward 89

OSBORNE, James 65
O'TOOLE, Edmund Joseph 57

PARKER, Charles Edward Haydon 115
PARSONS, Francis Newton 106
PHIPPS-HORNBY, Edmund John 113
PITTS, James 102
PRICE-DAVIES, Llewelyn Alberic Emilius 162

RAMSDEN, Horace Edward 81
RAVENHILL, George Albert 90

REED, Hamilton Lyster — 96
REYNOLDS, James Henry — 30
RICHARDSON, Arthur Herbert Lindsay — 125
ROBERTS, Frederick Hugh Sherston — 92
ROBERTSON, William — 78
ROGERS, James — 158

SHAUL, John David Francis — 84
SCHIESS, Christian Ferdinand — 36
SCHOFIELD, Harry Norton — 93
SCOTT, Robert — 103

TOWSE, Ernest Beachcroft Beckwith — 85
TRAYNOR, William Bernard — 151
TURNER, Richard Ernest William — 144

YOUNG, Alexander — 161
YOUNGER, David Reginald — 127

WASSALL, Samuel — 7
WARD, Charles Burley — 124
WILLIAMS (FIELDING), John — 27
WYLLY, Guy George Egerton — 139